CHRISTIANITY and the INTELLECTUALS

CHRISTIANITY and the INTELLECTUALS

Arther Trace

Sherwood Sugden & Company
PUBLISHERS

1117 Eighth Street, La Salle, Illinois 61301

ISBN 0-89385-018-7

First Edition

Copyright © 1983, Arther Trace

No part of this book may be reproduced, stored in a retrieval system, or transmitted in any form or by any means, electronic, mechanical, photocopy, or otherwise (excepting brief passages for purposes of review) without the prior written permission of the publisher:

Sherwood Sugden & Company, Publishers
1117 Eighth Street
La Salle, Illinois 61301

CONTENTS

I. How Influential Are Intellectuals?	7
II. Early Christian Intellectuals	18
III. The Phenomenon of Christian Humanism	45
IV. The De-Christianizing of the Intellectuals	67
V. The Rise of the Anti-Theists	93
VI. The De-Christianizing of American Intellectuals	122
VII. Solidifying the Post-Christian Age	137
VIII. Christian Intellectuals in a Post-Christian Age	171
IX. Where Now?	191
Index	200

CHAPTER I

HOW INFLUENTIAL ARE INTELLECTUALS?

This book proposes to describe the running epistemological war which the intellectuals have been fighting with Christianity and Christianity with the intellectuals almost from the beginning and which sometimes seemed resolved but at most times unresolvable. Basically the problem is this: Can unaided human faculties answer adequately the ultimate questions about human existence or can only the truths of Revelation answer them? And ultimately is there such a thing as Revelation?

At one extreme is the fideist or Christian antihumanist position which insists that the only important truths are God's truths revealed through Sacred Scripture, that whatever truths mere human faculties can discover are superfluous if not false or downright dangerous, and that no human faculties are adequate to answer the ultimate questions. The other extreme is the humanist anti-Christian position, which is an atheistic position, and which holds that there is no revelation, that what passes for Sacred Scripture is merely history and philosophy and poetry and is therefore susceptible to all the limitations of any other history or philosophy or poetry. In this view, the answers to the ultimate questions must come from the word of man because God didn't give man the Word, even if there were a God.

As a matter of fact, these extremes have already been represented in nearly pure form in Western civilization, the fideistic or Christian anti-humanist position in the early Christian era, and the atheistic or the humanistic anti-Christian position in the post-Christian era. In the intervening centuries, Christianity and humanism have been mixed in varying proportions with the greatest harmony coming during the Renaissance in the form of what is properly called Christian humanism. But this balance between human knowledge and divine knowledge was so precarious that it lasted little more than three centuries, from the middle of the 14th to the middle of the 17th, depending upon the country, and that balance has not been achieved either before or since.

The difficulty is that Christianity is an intellectual religion to a degree far beyond any other major religion, including Buddhism, Hinduism, Judaism, or Mohammedanism, and its doctrines, therefore, have been subjected to human scrutiny far more intensely than those of any other major religion. The utmost importance attaches to this phenomenon because so long as the doctrines of Christianity coincide with human understanding, Christianity is bound to benefit; but whenever human understanding runs counter to the authority of Christian doctrine, then Christianity tends to lose its authority because the vanity of mankind, including intellectuals, permits itself to believe that the truths of men are truer than the truths of God, and even to question whether there is a God.

The true triumph over the authority of religion and revelation was achieved by the philosophers in the 18th century and by the scientists in the 19th and 20th centuries. The last three centuries, consequently, have seen the steady and nearly complete de-Christianization of the intellectuals as learning passed from churchmen to non-churchmen to anti-churchmen. Today Christian intellectuals, as a result, have become not only rare but increasingly ineffectual.

But the attempt to substitute the authority of reason and science for the authority of religion appears to have posed problems which neither the 18th-century Enlighteners nor the 19th- and 20th-century scientific humanists had anticipated. The chief of these is the growing realization that neither reason nor science can provide the ultimate answers to the ultimate questions about human existence. In fact, sophisticated intellectuals are now coming to recognize that there is a great deal about the nature of man and indeed of the universe that will always be beyond the reach of reason and science; some are even concluding that there is nowhere to go except back to religion for an explanation of the meaning of existence. Furthermore, the spiritual nature of man, which 19th- and 20th-century intellectuals tend to deny as a matter of course, is once again being reaffirmed, even by some highly influential scientists. As a result, the concepts of the soul, of immortality, and of the world of the spirit are gaining respectability among respectable intellectuals who have perceived the fatal limitations of unaided human faculties as the way to the ultimate truths.

This is not to say that influential intellectuals are now ready to re-embrace the Christian view of the nature and destiny of man or to welcome back the mysteries of the Christian faith. Most major intellectuals are still hostile toward revealed religion where they are not indifferent to it. But this study will suggest that the direction which intellectual inquiry is now beginning to take indicates that intellectuals may turn once again to religion in the decades ahead.

It would be too much of a luxury to write a book about intellectuals without explaining what I mean by an intellectual. One of the simplest definitions is that an intellectual is someone who gets excited about ideas. Not many people become very excited about ideas for very long, especially if an "idea" is defined in the philosophical sense as "a concept of abstract truth or reason." And yet I shall think of the intellectual as one who is given to speculating, preferably in fairly systematic fashion, about abstract truths, especially about "final causes," to use Aristotle's phrase, or questions of "ultimate concern," to use Paul Tillich's phrase, or questions like "What's it all for?" to use a popular phrase.

The most readily identifiable intellectuals are those who have demonstrated their interest in ideas through publication of some sort, since that is likely to be the most accessible record of what most of them thought. An intellectual does not necessarily have to be a theologian or a philosopher; he can be an historian, a poet, a novelist, a dramatist, or even a scientist or a social scientist. He can indeed be anyone who is devoted to studying and pursuing ideas. The intellectual today is most likely to be found in the university, though perhaps upwards of 75 per cent of the professors in most universities are not intellectuals as I shall think of an intellectual. Occasionally he may be found in government, in the non-academic professions, in publishing, in the mass-culture industries, in science laboratories, or if in none of these then perhaps in his study, if he can afford one. During the Middle Ages he was found almost exclusively in the monasteries and the churches, but today he will be found there as if by accident.

It is not enough for an intellectual to be learned, though it is best that he be so. Scholars, for example, are not *ipso facto* intellectuals, for scholars may be too dedicated to the fact and not enough to the idea. Facts are more or less verifiable, whereas genuine ideas are not, at least not in any scientific or systematic way. Indeed one reason why ideas can be so powerful is that they cannot be easily disproved. Some of the most important and far-reaching ideas in the history of civilization are the least verifiable.

The best intellectuals have not merely acquisitive and analytical minds but also critical, imaginative, and creative minds. They tend therefore to be disturbers of the *status quo*, especially insofar as they would often like to see their own ideas replace someone else's. They can do much both to create intellectual tradition and to destory it, but their role is no less to preserve it wherever they felt that it should be preserved, and they become skilled at relating topical truths to higher truths.

In the beginning the intellectual may be a relatively dispassionate searcher after truth, but characteristically when he thinks he has discovered the truth he is transformed into an ideologue, i.e., he becomes at least tentatively committed to the truth of a particular idea or set of ideas to the exclusion of other or contrary ideas. In time he may even come to feel that his search for the truth has ended. The alternative may be to discover on his deathbed that in his lifelong quest he still cannot decide whether one idea is nearer the truth than any other.

As truth-seekers, intellectuals seek the truth in various ways: Some seek it primarily through Revelation (religion), some primarily through reason (philosophy), some primarily through the imagination (poetry, drama, fiction), some primarily through the memory (history), and some through the senses (science). There are, of course, many other methods, but these are the traditional and the most widely recognized methods of arriving at truth. Those who seek it through Revelation, however, differ from all the rest because they place their ultimate trust in God's word, whereas the others place their trust in man's word. It is precisely this difference which I should like to explore in this study, more specifically the difference between those who find the highest truths in the Bible and Christian doctrine and those who find them through exclusively secular authority.

This study is proceeding on the premise that as intellectuals go, so goes Christianity, that in time, the intellectual climate profoundly affects the non-intellectual climate, and that therefore unbelievers among the intellectuals breed unbelievers among the non-intellectuals. And yet this premise may be sharply challenged because it may by no means be evident that the world's mighty minds have all that much influence on unmighty minds in matters of religion or anything else. Voltaire once observed that "If we divide mankind into twenty parts, it will be found that nineteen of these consist of persons employed in manual labor, who will never know that such a man as Mr. Locke existed. In the remaining twentieth part, how few readers! And among such as are so, twenty amuse themselves with romances to one who studies philosophy. The thinking part of mankind are confined to a very small number, and those will never disturb the peace and tranquillity of the world." "All the works of the modern philosophers put together," he concluded, "will never make so much noise as even the dispute which arose from the Franciscans, merely about the fashion of their sleeves and of their cowls."

It may be that Voltaire was not serious in these observations, just as he was not serious in many others, for he knew as well as any other giant intellectual that ideas have consequences, even beyond imagination; and it is no small irony that the latter part of the 18th century is commonly called the Age of Voltaire. Still, it must be admitted at the outset that any effort to estimate the influence of intellectuals on non-intellectuals is a risky business, for the influence of intellectuals works in subtle and largely unmeasurable ways.

For this reason it is just as possible to take the position that the most influential of "the thinking part of mankind," who may be even fewer than Voltaire estimated, have not only disturbed "the peace and tranquility of the world" from time to time, but have caused ideological upheavals and intellectual earthquakes which have shaken whole nations to their foundations. A seemingly clear-cut instance of the powerful influence of the intellectual is the fact that the Soviet government rules in the name of a single individual, Karl Marx, who spent most of his life in libraries and whose works over the past century have been studied by countless other intellectuals. In turn, *Das Capital* did not spring from Marx's head spontaneously, for what he was doing in all those years in the libraries of Europe was reading the works and absorbing the thinking of a good many other intellectuals, ranging from Democritus and Epicurus, whose works were the subject of his dissertation, to Hegel and Saint-Simon and Feuerbach. There is perhaps no more poignant example of how an intellectual who was influenced by other intellectuals and who in turn influenced still other intellectuals—finally reaches down into the daily life of even the most remote peasant. Something of the same process led to the sudden communization of China and thus profoundly affected the thinking and daily lives of a billion more people.

Similarly, it is not possible to imagine that the Reformation could have taken place without the leadership of intellectuals. Most religious movements are the consequence of the efforts of a single religious leader, or at most a few, and the Reformation was no different. It was not a gradual groundswell of vast armies of discontented non-intellectuals who brought about the Reformation. It was thinking and writing, especially of Luther, Calvin, and Zwingli, along with a few others, around whom the people, to be sure, rallied in breaking away from the Roman Catholic Church, but without whom it is difficult to imagine that the Reformation, at least in anything like the proportions it was to assume, could have taken place.

Other and perhaps not less dramatic examples could be cited of revolutions and movements, social, political, and cultural, which are more or less directly traceable to the influence of a few intellectuals, the French and American revolutions among them. But generally the influence of ideas and of intellectuals works in far more subtle fashion, so subtle, in fact, that it is not always easy to identify either the idea or the intellectual. When one recognizes, for example, that Aristotle may have had something to do with the fact that Catholic priests are allowed to drink whiskey and that Plato may have had something to do with the fact that Seventh Day Adventists are not allowed to drink coffee, one begins to understand a little about how the influence of intellectuals, however deviously, may reach down even into the living room, to say nothing of the bedroom.

What kind of ideas in the long run exert the greatest influence on civilization? In particular, what kind of ideas have done the most to unify what is called Western Civilization during, say, the last 1500 years? Lord Keynes, the British economist, who held a far different view of the influence of intellectuals than Voltaire, observed once that "The ideas of economists and political philosophers, both when they are right and when they are wrong, are more powerful than is commonly understood. Indeed, the world is ruled by little else." And yet the most powerful ideas in Western Civilization appear not to have been political or economic or indeed scientific ideas, because none of these kinds of ideas have prevailed for very long. One political or economic or scientific idea is too soon replaced by another that may even contradict the one it replaced. What 20th-century America has in common, for example, with 12th-century Europe is not surely a common bond of political and economic beliefs, for the economic and political premises of these two centuries could hardly be more different.

But what they do have in common are certain religious and moral ideas and ideals, which, however eroded they have become in our own century, are still very much with us; and this common bond is due to the fact that these ideas come from the same source: the Bible and Christian tradition. These ideals have in fact been shared to a greater or lesser degree by most of Western Civilization for at least the past thousand years and much of it for some five hundred years before that. They have thrived because they enjoyed the support of the intellectuals, and the reason their influence is eroding in the 20th century is that they no longer have the support of the intellectuals.

It is not easy to predict how different Western Civilization would have been if Augustine, Jerome, Athanasius, Bernard, Abelard, and Thomas Aquinas and their disciples had been the great unbelievers of the Western World and if Voltaire, Rousseau, Kant, Hegel, Bentham, Nietzsche, Marx, Freud, Dewey, and Sartre and their disciples had been the great believers; but one can perhaps at least as justifiably presume that it would have been very different as to assume that it would be no different. It all depends upon one's understanding of how powerful or powerless ideas are in determining the course of history.

But if one scans the history of Western Civilization, or Eastern Civilization for that matter, no ideas appear to have affected the thought and behavior—and condition—of more people for longer periods than religious ideas. Christ, for example, appears to have more profoundly affected the lives of more people, both intellectuals and non-intellectuals, than any other intellectual or any political or military leader in the Western World that one can name. Alongside that of Christ, the influence of Alexander the Great or Napoleon or Hitler or Stalin, or even Plato or Aristotle or Marx or any scientist or poet or intellectual of any kind seems small. Merely the number of times that hundreds of millions of Christians during the course of the last 2,000 years have gone to church in Christ's name is enough to make the influence of any other intellectual or non-intellectual seem insignificant. And when one tries to imagine the influence that Christ has had and is still having on the daily lives of hundreds of millions of people in what they have done and have refrained from doing in accordance with the teachings of Christianity, one can get some understanding of how powerful religious ideas can be. And when one adds to Chrsit's influence the influence of Buddha, Moses, and Mohammed, compared to the influence of anybody else, the understanding can become even clearer that no ideas are so powerful as religious ideas, even today.

And yet Christianity in the 20th century is being besieged as never before by anti-religious ideas so that one has to wonder whether Christianity may not in time cease to be a consequential force in the world. The assault by intellectuals on Christianity has been going on for more than two centuries but so gradually that it is difficult to pinpoint at any given time how seriously Christianity has lost its influence in the history of the Western World. One thing that is certain, however, is that in the history of Western Civilization since the time of Christ, most of the intellectuals up to the end of the Renaissance were Christians, whereas most of the intellectuals since the Rennaisance were not and are not now. This loss of religious faith may turn out to be one of the most important phenomena in the history of Western Civilization. The aim of this study, then, is to attempt to account for this loss of faith.

CHAPTER II

EARLY CHRISTIAN INTELLECTUALS

In a sense, the first intellectuals of any civilization were those who specialized in religious principles and practices. It was they who engaged in the loftiest speculations and who were regarded as the founts or at least the trustees of the highest wisdom. It was they who passed on the doctrine and lore of religion to succeeding generations and to whom everyone looked for the final word about the final questions. The advent of written language and the subsequent appearance of Sacred Scriptures solidified the role of the religious intellectual as truth-bearer, whether the religion was Buddhism, Hinduism, Judaism, Christianity, or Mohammedanism. The most learned men in these civilizations were in the beginning the priests and rabbis and monks whose duty it was to know what the Sacred Scriptures said and what they meant. In other words, the first intellectuals were thoroughly religionized because by more or less universal consent the highest truths were religious truths and the ultimate source of truth of the great religions was to be found in the sacred writings on which they were based.

The development of the Christian intellectual tradition, however, did not come easily, for Christianity grew out of the civilizations of ancient Greece and Rome as well as the civilizations of the Eastern Mediterranean. And so in the early centuries of the Christian era, the competition from non-Christian intellectuals was so strong as to be almost overwhelming. It is true that the Golden Age of Roman thought and letters with such brilliant intellectuals as Virgil, Horace, Cicero, and Livy had gone, but the earliest Christian era under the name of the Silver Age in Rome could still produce spectacular non-Christian intellectuals like Lucan, Petronius, Seneca, the Plinys, Tacitus, and Quintilian, thus continuing a strong intellectual pagan tradition in the West that seriously challenged the efforts of Christianity to establish its own intellectual tradition. Furthermore, Christianity had hitherto found stiff competition from the mystical religions such as those of Isis in Egypt, Judaism in the Near East, and Mithraism, which had been spreading westward from Persia. And paganism even to the end of the 4th century A.D. was ardently defended by Roman and Greek academics, and strengthened by the influence of Stoicism and Neoplatonism, which, like Christianity, reflected a monotheistic religion.

Yet pagan thought, not only in the Greek world but to some extent in the Roman world of the first two centuries of the Christian era was in a sense religious or at least concerned with the highest moral ideas. By this time the Skeptics and the Epicureans, who represented the least spiritual strains of pagan philosophy, were widely rejected. The tenor of philosophical thought during this period was far better reflected in the moral, even spiritual thought of Marcus Aurelius, Epictetus, and Plutarch, and especially the neo-Platonism of Plotinus, who was the last of the great pagan philosophers. Together they did much to bridge the gap between the pagan world and the Christian world, between philosophy and religion.

As the Christian world expanded, the Christianization of the intellectuals became inevitable. By the time of

Emperor Constantine in the early 4th century perhaps 30 percent of the urban population was Christian. This fact is important because, as always, intellectuals tend to congregate in the cities; and since Christianity was a highly literate religion it had a peculiar attraction for highly educated men, including many of the best minds of the late Roman Empire. And to the extent that it absorbed classical thought and culture, it carried on the best intellectual traditions. Yet it would not perhaps have triumphed, at least not so soon, without the support of the emperors, which is one reason why the conversion of Constantine in 312 was so important to its future and so instrumental in Christianizing the intellectuals. Julian the Apostate, it is true, almost undid what Constantine had done by reverting to paganism and inviting his subjects to do the same; but the growth of Christianity could not be stopped, nor could its eventual control of learning.

Partly in reaction to the anarchic threats of Gnosticism, which tended to teach that knowledge could be communicated directly from God to men without an interpreter, the early Christian Church established a strong hierarchy, whose authority was not only administrative but doctrinal. And it thus recognized that its leaders must be learned. As a result, by the end of the 4th century the most powerful intellectuals in Europe were Christian intellectuals. A whole galaxy of them appeared very early in the Church's history, including Clement, Origen, Tertullian, Cyprian, Irenaeus, and Hippolytus in the second and third centuries; and Athanasius, Basil, Chrysostom, Hilary, Gregory of Nyssa, Jerome, and Augustine in the 4th and 5th centuries. It was such intellectuals who laid the foundations upon which Christianity was to be the wave of the future and paganism the wave of the past; their writings were far more influential than those of any contemporary pagan writers. In fact, by the 6th century almost all the literate men in Europe were Christians and virtually all the important works in the late Empire, whether in Greek or Latin, were from the pens of Christian intellectuals. Augustine himself became easily the most influential intellectual of them all in that, more than any other single writer, he determined the tone and indeed the direction of Christianity for the next eight centuries.

And yet it cannot be said that the Church hastened to train Christian intellectuals. Even after Constantine's conversion most branches of learning were still in pagan hands and they remained so up until the fall of the Western Empire. The Church had established no schools, no academies, no universities. Even in the Eastern Empire, where Christianity spread much faster, learning remained under the supervision of the state. There were great universities in Alexandria, Athens, Constantinople, and Antioch; and in the 4th and 5th centuries schools of medicine, philosophy, literature and rhetoric more or less thrived, but they were all pagan. Finally, in the early 6th century, Justinian in a fit of piety closed them all down, seized the property, and brought an end to eleven centuries' accumulation of Greek learning.

But even in the West, after the collapse of the public system of education, the Church made no move to reform education, much less to control it. The learned layman Cassiodorus suggested to Pope Agapetus in 536 that Christian schools be established in Rome, but war put an end to the project. Cassiodorus did, however, manage to set up a Christian school in southern Italy where monks and learned laymen could copy manuscripts of secular texts for religious purposes. And following Augustine's plan, he developed a course of study, both religious and secular, for Christian monasteries.

The efforts to theologize learning succeeded at last when Isadore, Bishop of Seville, made public in the year 636 his *Etymologies*, which was a vast compendium of human knowledge, including the seven liberal arts, the subsidiary arts of medicine and law, the interpretation of the Bible, and the role of the Church. The *Etymologies* was like an intellectual wheel whose hub was Christian doctrine and whose spokes reached out into every area of human knowledge. It became the basis of all teaching in the West, and so did much to guarantee that students and intellectuals for centuries to come would acquire their learning in a Christian context.

As Christianity entered the early Middle Ages, i.e., about 500 A.D., learning had reached nearly its lowest level, and the barbarian invasions did not help. Indeed the barbarians enjoyed an outstanding record, especially in the terrible 9th century, of destroying cities, libraries, schools, and other repositories of wisdom, and otherwise interfered with the progress of intellectual life. The only means by which learning could be preserved during these centuries was through the monasteries. By the 8th century, virtually all the learning and the learned in Christendom were in one way or another connected with the Church and depended upon the Church. The monasteries were the chief centers of learning from the 6th to the 12th centuries, and without them learning would have become extinct in Western Europe. Perhaps 90 percent of the literate men between 600 and 1100 were educated in monastic schools. The Benedictine monasteries did the most for learning during these centuries, and by the year 800 they had been established all over Europe. The most important ones had flourishing schools, large libraries, and *scriptoria* for the production of manuscripts.

Monks were transcribing manuscripts as early as the late 4th century under the auspices of Gregory of

Tours, but Cassiodorus's school in Italy became the model *scriptorium* for most monasteries. Far more time, however, was devoted to copying the works of the early Church Fathers, especially Ambrose, Jerome, Augustine, and Gregory the Great, and making copies of the Bible and the saints' lives; less time was spent copying the Greek and Latin pagan classics. The activities of the *scriptoria* reached their peak in the 7th and 8th centuries, particularly in England and Ireland, where the monks were the most learned and where their contribution to learning was the greatest.

But the monasteries were not universities. There was little opportunity for intellectual speculation and interchange of ideas. In fact, the purpose of the monasteries was not to perfect the mind but to perfect the soul, and so they produced no intellectuals of the order of Jerome or Augustine. They did, however, produce, for example, the Venerable Bede, whose intellect was sufficiently powerful that his works, too, were widely copied in the *scriptoria*. The monasteries also produced Johannes Scotus Erigena or "John the Irishman," whose learning was reflected in a prodigious work, *The Division of the Universe*, which was an attempt to formulate a theological theory of the creation and the origin of the universe. And they produced the most learned man of the time, Alcuin, who became the chief cultural and religious advisor to Charlemagne, so that his influence reached farther, perhaps, than that of any other Christian intellectual since Augustine.

And yet the early Middle Ages was, on balance, a period of depressed intellectual activity which seemed to have grown out of a sense of inferiority, a feeling that the early Chruch Fathers had said all that there was to say about Christianity, that the Church was the final arbiter in any case, and that secular learning could never again rise to the height that it had achieved among the ancient

Greeks and Romans. During the second half of the 12th century the monasteries underwent a rapid decline, and learning then passed to the cathedral schools, particularly in northern France at Chartres and Orleans, which became seats of classical learning, and at Rheims and Lyon, which became centers of scholastic learning. Canterbury Cathedral became a major center of learning in England and the cathedral in Toledo became another in Spain. These schools, though always under church auspices, contributed much to the advancement of learning, especially during the 12th century. Many of the greatest writers of that century, whether in theology or philosophy, were in one way or another associated with the cathedral schools, including bishops such as Peter Lombard at Paris and John of Salisbury at Chartres, chancellors such as Anselm of Laon and Bernard of Chartres, and cathedral teachers such as Bernard Sylvester and Peter Abelard—Christian intellectuals all, and of the highest order.

Out of the cathedral schools grew the great medieval universities, most of which were founded in the 12th century. The names of Abelard, St. Bernard, and John of Salisbury were associated with them at that stage as portents of the rapid intellectual growth to come. In the 13th century the universities, such as those at Paris, Oxford, Montpelier, Bologna, and Salerno, became the intellectual centers of Europe. Relative to the 10th and 11th centuries, the 12th and particularly the 13th experienced an explosion of knowledge, not only in philosophy and theology, but in science, history, government, and many other fields. The 13th century was in fact the century of the great medieval surveys of human knowledge, the chief example of which was the enormous *Speculum Maius* of the Dominican scholar Vincent of Beauvais. It was equal to 40 modern volumes and became the standard encyclopedia for the remainder of the Middle Ages.

Some of the universities, unlike the cathedral schools, were not born under the paternal watchfulness of the Church. They tended to evolve haphazardly, but as their intellectual influence increased, they not only became answerable to the Church; they were directed by the Church. In England, education in the universities as in the schools was wholly under the control of the Church. The schools were in fact her adjuncts; the schoolmasters were ecclesiastical officers; and the Church courts held full jurisdiction over schools and universities alike. In fact, until 1540, all schoolmasters, professors and scholars were in religious orders, however minor. Virtually the same situation prevailed on the continent, except that in Italy some grammar schools, as holdovers from imperial times, maintained a secular status. Even during the lifetimes of St. Francis and St. Dominic the friars began to settle at the universities and hence to exert a powerful Christian influence upon the intellectual life, especially at Bologna and Paris and Oxford. Actually some of the most influential intellectuals of the 13th and 14th centuries were friars, as, for example, Bonaventura, Duns Scotus, and William of Ockham among the Franciscans, and Albertus Magnus, Thomas Aquinas, and Johannes Eckhart among the Dominicans. It is not that most students who attended the universities wanted to become theologians; the fact is that most of them wanted to study law. But the point here is that learning at these universities took place in a Christian intellectual atmosphere, and Christian doctrine pretty thoroughly informed learning in whatever field.

All this is not to say that secular learning and religious learning were harmoniously intertwined during the 12th and 13th centuries, for the fact is that they were not. As might be expected, the greatest intellectual clashes in the heyday of the great medieval universities came between the philosophers and theologians, between those who made great claims for the authority of reason and those who more firmly insisted upon the authority of revelation. Out of such controversies attempts to reconcile classical thought with Christian doctrine reached new heights. The papacy had therefore always to keep an eye on the intellectual direction of the universities and from time to time would issue bulls against whatever intellectual currents seemed dangerous to the faith. There were many such, for Christian intellectuals were continually at each others' throats as philosophical speculation increased in intensity.

One of the problems was that Christian intellectuals in the 13th century turned in increasing numbers to Aristotle as the fount of pagan learning and human reason—with all the attendant risks. During the early Middle Ages, Christian intellectuals were attracted to Plato because in many ways his thought was compatible with Christian doctrine, particularly his position on immortality and his dim view of bodily appetites. But Aristotle's position on the crucial doctrine of immortality was not so compatible with Christian teaching, nor was his view of the creation and the eternity of the universe, which was not compatible with the Mohammedan or Jewish views either. Averroës, the great 12th-century Mohammedan philosopher, had set an example by sticking with Aristotle rather than with Mohammed, particularly in denying personal immortality, and his example inspired a whole school of heretical Christian thinkers.

In fact the whole grand debate over the nature of universals was now to be revived, and it served to dramatize the uneasy relationship between reason and religion as the age of the medieval universities began. The realist faction, which insisted that reality belongs only to the idea or the universal and that particulars are mere phantasms, raised embarrassing questions about personal immortality and even about the personality of God as well as the personality of man. The nominalists, on the other hand, who held that reality exists only in particulars, challenged the existence of the Trinity and in effect seemed to make Christianity a polytheistic religion. Needless to say, the Church was a bit touchy on the procedure of applying scholastic philosophy to Christian doctrine, as the case of Abelard eloquently testified.

In any event, the 13th century saw scholastic thought at its height as an outgrowth of the increasing influence of Aristotle, and it produced the greatest scholastic of them all, Thomas Aquinas. Aquinas made his intellectual headquarters in the University of Paris and in due time produced his great *Summa Theologiae*, which succeeded in reconciling Aristotelian thought with Christian doctrine far better than had ever been done before or was ever to be done again.

The greatest intellectual activity in Western Europe was in fact taking place at the University of Paris, which drew the most radical thinkers, the hottest debaters, the sharpest dialecticians, and the most dangerous heretics. Even the genius of Aquinas did not satisfy every intellectual on the crucial question of fusing reason with revelation. Indeed, at first he satisfied almost no one. The Averroists thought that he was not radical enough and that he had in fact perverted Aristotelian thought in order to preserve Christian doctrine, and the Augustinians objected that he had given away too much fundamental Christian doctrine in order to accommodate Aristotle and therefore concluded that much of his thought smacked of heresy.

The intellectual clashes between the philosophers

and the theologians at the University of Paris in the 13th century merely reflect the fact that throughout the whole history of intellectual activity in the medieval Christian world, the most compelling question was the extent to which pagan learning could be made compatible with Christian doctrine, which is another way of inquiring whether the truths of reason could be made compatible with the truths of Revelation after all. The civilizations of Greece and Rome had produced great reasoners, and Christianity had produced great believers. No Christian denied that the great mysteries of Christianity contradicted the dictates of reason and common experience, which is why they were mysteries. That is also why the 2nd-century Church Father Tertullian, a learned man of great faith, exclaimed, "I believe because it is absurd," and why Augustine insisted that "the authority of the Scripture is higher than all the efforts of human intelligence."

And yet since classical learning represented the highest efforts of human intelligence it was hard to ignore. Men were given minds to reason with, memories to remember, imaginations to imagine, and eyes and ears to see and hear; and the most thoughtful of them are going to strike out on their own with them in quest of the truth and to pursue that truth wherever it leads regardless of whether or not it coincides with what their religion tells them. Tertullian was quite aware of the dangers that the veneration of classical learning might pose to Christianity, and, though thoroughly conversant with it himself, he ultimately concluded that Christians should reject it utterly. "What is there in common," he asked, "between Athens and Jerusalem, between the academy and the Church? For us we have no need for curiosity after Jesus Christ, or for investigation after the Gospel."

Jerome, on the other hand, was of a different mind. It is true that one time in a dream he imagined that at the

Judgement Day the Judge condemned him to Hell because he followed Cicero too much and Christ too little, and that the Judge relented only after Jerome promised to read henceforth only the books of God and not the books of man. But his position is more nearly typified by his answer to the charge that in his continual quoting of pagan authors he was "defiling the whiteness of the Church with the foulness of heathenism." "My efforts," he replied, "promote the advantage of Christ's family, my so-called defilement with an alien increases the number of my fellow-servants." Clearly Jerome thought that the pagan writers could strengthen Christian belief. But Jerome's view posed problems of the most serious sort, for the reconciliation of pagan learning with Christian doctrine was fraught with such difficulties that at times it seemed impossible, or worse, it led to the preference for human knowledge over divine knowledge.

In the third century an attempt at solving the problem was made by the Alexandrian theologian Origen, who introduced the "double-faith" concept which held that there was a simple faith for ignorant Christians and a sophisticated philosophical body of doctrines for learned Christians. Most of the early Church Fathers, including Augustine, subscribed to the double-faith concept, though often after much soul-searching. The study of pagan thought by Christian intellectuals seemed therefore to be duly sanctioned. And so, inspired by the efforts of the Jewish philosopher Philo, who attempted a reconciliation of Platonism and Judaism, many of the early Church Fathers undertook to reconcile pagan thought with Christian doctrine. But for centuries the reconciliation made little headway, even though virtually all of the great Christian intellectuals of the early and medieval Church were thoroughly acquainted with classical thought as well as Christian thought.

The fact is that during the first twelve centuries of Christianity the spirit of fideism pretty thoroughly dominated Christian intellectual life. There was no consensus that Christian doctrine and pagan philosophy could be readily fused. The faculty of reason was mistrusted almost as much as the imagination and the senses. St. Augustine had said, "I believe in order that I may understand," in the 4th century, and St. Anselm was still saying it in the 12th.

But even in the 15th century the Chancellor of the University of Paris, Jean Charlier de Gerson, who perceived that the philosophers and theologians in his university were tearing each other apart, asserted the supremacy of Revelation over reason. "Let us make use of Reason solely in order to arrive at the truth, which it cannot do without the aid of Faith. It is the rule of Faith that we need follow, and if some refractory and stubborn minds still cling to the quibbles of philosophy, let us deplore their being led astray, and humbly seek in the bosom of the Church, far from the schools, peace, light, and life." So said the head of the chief center of learning in Europe.

The Chancellor may well not have been speaking for a good many of the radicals and dissidents in his university, but even they in the early 15th century were far from denying that the Bible was the word of God, that Christ was their Savior, and that many, if not all, of the fundamental doctrines of the Christian Church were true. However much their reason impinged upon their religion, the overwhelming majority of the intellectuals in the Middle Ages were Christian intellectuals, which meant that they exercised their minds within the confines of the fundamental doctrines of Christianity.

But some of the "refractory and stubborn minds" of the sort that the Chancellor of Paris referred to were also among the most powerful minds in Europe, even while the Church was in its infancy. Some of these powerful minds were in fact among the Church's most formidable heretics. I should like to consider briefly some of the great heretics of the Early Church as a way of dramatizing the problems posed by the clash between the authority of God and the authority of man in the early Christian world.

"Do not think that heresies could have arisen from a few beggarly little souls," said Augustine, "only great men have brought forth heresies." Such was indeed the case—not only in Augustine's time but afterwards as well. But the great heretics in the history of Christianity were remarkable quite as much for the intensity of their faith as for the power of their minds. Essentially they were religious reformers. They were not unbelievers; on the contrary, they tended to be fanatics. They were more Christian than the Christians, and though their aim was to purify the Church, they sometimes came close to destroying it. The best heretical intellectuals were quite as concerned with ultimate truths as the best orthodox intellectuals; and it must be said too that, however paradoxically, they performed a necessary function by causing orthodox churchmen constantly to define and redefine what orthodoxy was.

The earliest intellectual troublers of the infant Church were the Gnostics, who produced a swarm of heresies that were to plague the Church for centuries to come. Having already incorporated Hellenism and Orientalism as well as elements of Judaism into their thinking, they also incorporated Christianity, and thought in fact that with all their anterior knowledge they were improving Christianity. But the Gnostics provided such free-wheeling interpretations of fundamental Christian doctrine that the Fathers of the Church felt that they had no recourse but to refute them, if not to persecute them. The idea, for example, that Christ did not really appear on earth in corporal form and that He therefore did not even "die" was found to be intolerable, since the Incarnation is central to Christianity, to say nothing of the Crucifixion and the Resurrection. But their position on the Incarnation was compatible with their position that all matter is evil, so evil in fact, that the creator of the world was not the true God, who would never have performed so nasty a deed, but rather a demiurge, an inferior deity who has been put in charge of the material world. Their bizarre interpretation of the Scriptures also proved intolerable, especially those who exalted Judas Iscariot as the instrument of redemption and even Adam's and Eve's serpent as the instrument of human knowledge. In their seeming perverseness, some of them also defended Cain and the Sodomites and rejected Abel, Enoch, and Noah.

Gnosticism appeared in many guises in the early centuries of Christianity, but it presents some choice examples of the early clashes between the intellectuals and the Church. One of the earliest conflicts between heretical intellectuals and the early Church was created by the radical reformer, Marcion, who was born about the year 85 A.D. Marcion started out as a shipbuilder, but in time turned into an intellectual. In his new role as thinker he found that he had to reject the Old Testament *in toto* because it presented an erroneous notion of God. He rejected the Gospel of St. Matthew because it referred too often to the Old Testament, and he rejected the Gospel of Mark because there were too few of the sayings of Jesus. He also found the Gospel of John to be contaminated because it stated that salvation came from the Jews. This left him with the Gospel of Luke, with which he could find almost no fault, though he also did away with the pastoral letters of Paul and rejected many of his remaining letters.

In addition to reforming the Scriptures, Marcion also sought to reform the Church, which he felt was relapsing into Judaism because it did not distinguish sufficiently between the Gospel and the Law. For his pains he was expelled from the Christian community in Rome in the year 144 as a heretic. In retaliation he founded his own church to directly rival the official Church, even though its members were required to abstain from meat, wine, and sex and to be prepared for martyrdom at any moment. Marcionite churches by the year 150 sprang up everywhere, and some of his followers did find the opportunity for martyrdom. None of Marcion's writings, however, have survived, for they were all effectively destroyed by the Church.

One of the most brilliant heretics of the very early Church was Origen, who illustrates perhaps even more dramatically the problem of a religious philosopher who strikes his intellectual sword against the rock of orthodoxy. Origen was so zealous that in a sudden fit of piety he made himself a eunuch in accordance with a suggestion in Matthew 19:12. He was later tutored and taught to think by no less a person than Clement of Alexandria, one of the greatest of all the patristic writers. Clement turned him into a first-class intellectual. Whereas in his earlier life Origen had found philosophy to be so evil that he burned his secular library, he now came to regard it as simply another road to God, and so he took it up again. He studied Greek philosophy in order to make himself and others better Christians. But as a philosophizing Christian he developed some ideas of his own which, as it turned out, the Church could not brook, including the idea of universal salvation, the eventual redemption of Satan and the temporal nature of Hell, all on the grounds that God's mercy is greater than He has been given credit for. He suffered martyrdom at the hands of Emperor Decius in A.D. 250, who imprisoned and maltreated him not because he was a heretic but because he was a Christian. But the Christians got to him even before Decius did on account of his deviations from orthodoxy; for as his fame grew, so did the number of his enemies. He was driven from the Christian community in Alexandria, and was even charged with being an unworthy priest on the grounds that he was a eunuch. After his death, he was repeatedly denounced, often by his students, as a blasphemer, an apostate, and a pagan, until finally in the year 543, some three centuries after his death, a synod at Constantiniple, at the insistence of Emperor Justinian, anathematized him, and ten years later his doctrines were officially condemned.

Another heretic in the early centuries of Christianity whose mind posed a substantial threat to the Church was Montanus, who called for a revival of first-century Christian zeal. He not only claimed that further revelation, indeed continuous revelation, was forthcoming, but that he himself was that paraclete predicted in the Gospel of John and that he had something to reveal. What he had to reveal was that the world was coming to an end. The Church had been trying to forget that it too had preached that doctrine, and it did not like to hear it so convincingly preached again because it caused so much discomfort. In advocating a return to the spirit of the primitive Church, Montanus had also come out against food and flesh and in favor of mortification and martyrdom. But the Church declared Montanus to be a pseudo-prophet and excommunicated him and his followers, thus creating one of the first great schisms. Montanus even succeeded in snaring the great Tertullian, who had hitherto been an archenemy of heresies, and he also inspired a good many of his followers to become martyrs.

Still another of the earliest heretics whose independent thinking seriously threatened the authority of the Church was Donatus, Bishop of Carthage, who was endowed with uncanny intellectual as well as spiritual gifts. In his zeal he reasoned that the sacraments were not valid when administered by priests in a state of sin. The Church in its own zeal, however, and in its knowledge of human nature, perceived the danger of linking its future to the personal virtue of its priests, and so declared Donatus a heretic. His fellow heretics were fined, their property confiscated, and some were even led to mass suicide. Nonetheless, they succeeded in spreading themselves all across North Africa, and except for a period between 700 and 1150 when they were dormant, they remained a threat to the Church from the 4th to the 16th centuries.

Meanwhile Pelagius, a monk from Britain, or more likely Ireland, rocked the whole Christian world with the notion that Adam and Eve did not pass on their Original Sin to posterity. This conclusion caused such a stir among churchmen that Pelagius had to go to Africa to discuss his doctrine with the greatest churchman of them all, St. Augustine. By this time Augustine had quit supporting heresies and started fighting them. He was not pleased with Pelagius, and after his views were discussed by a number of councils, Augustine engineered his excommunication. This development drew him to the East, where he was expelled from Jerusalem on account of his doctrines. Where he went thereafter no one knows, but his followers continued to threaten the authority of the Church for some time after.

By the 4th century the Church had assigned great councils to deal with the great intellectuals who had become great heretics. One of these was Arius, the

Presbyter of Alexandria, who probably got his education at the rationalistic school in Antioch. In any case, he became convinced that though Christ was indeed the Son of the Father, He was neither consubstantial nor coeternal with the Father. For this bit of reasoning Arius was removed from office and excommunicated and made the victim of a systematic campaign of slander. But his teachings caught on so well that the famous Council of Nicea (325), with the prodding of the famous bishop Athanasius, concluded that Arius's heresy was genuine. His writings were called up and he himself was banished to the hinterlands of Ilyria. But just as he was about to be restored to office he died. Bishop Athanasius, in perhaps a not wholly objective account, described the manner of his death. He records how on the day of his reinstallation Arius was walking along the street with his friend Bishop Eusebius when he was horribly riven by a seizure which caused not only his bowels and his liver to emerge from his body, but also his heart, whereupon he fell into a sewer and disappeared.

By this time virtually the whole Christian world had divided itself into Arians and Athanasians, and Athanasius no doubt hoped that the fact that a heretic should end up dead in a sewer would not be lost on the faithful. But many came to Arius's figurative rescue, including the Emperor Constantius, and his heresy prospered and grew into a great church in its own right. Nor was the controversy between Arius and Athanasius merely a polite theological debate: it ended in the slaughter of more Christians by other Christians (during the years 342-43) than by all the Roman pagans in history.

It is not possible to call the roll of all the intellectuals who became heretics in the history of the early Church. The aim here is merely to suggest the ease with which men's intellects can impinge upon their religion and seriously threaten it, if not destroy it. For there is little doubt that such heresies as Arianism, Montanism, Donatism, Pelagianism, to say nothing of such oriental heresies as Gnosticism and Manicheism, if they had prospered, would have brought the Church to its knees as soon as it was able to stand on its feet.

The church was obliged to rush to its own defense because it properly feared for its life. By way of reprisal it not only commonly excommunicated the offenders, but sent in its most distinguished Fathers to combat heresy wherever it could be found. Among them was Irenaeus, Bishop of Lyon, whose chief work entitled *Against the Heresies* (ca. 180 A.D.) was not only an exposé of Gnosticism, but the first systematic exposition of Christian belief. In the first half of the third century Hippolytus, one of the most learned of the early Roman Christians, and a disciple of Irenaeus, wrote a more comprehensive book entitled *Refutation of all Heresies*, in which he was able to trace all heresy to the attempt to reconcile Christianity with Greek philosophy.

One of the weapons of the Church against heresy was the practice of destroying all the heretical literature it could find, and it succeeded to the point that most of our knowledge of these heresies comes from those who attacked them, and hence it is often difficult to get a clear picture of their precise nature. But Hippolytus knew what he was about in observing that heresy is hydra-headed, for it was as if the destruction of one heresy led to the appearance of more.

Any consideration of the problem of intellectual freedom in the medieval Christian world ought probably to be accompanied by a consideration of the same problem in the Moslem and Jewish worlds, for the Christian record by comparison does not seem so bad. Mohammedanism, even Mohammed himself, appeared, it is true, to encourage the pursuit of knowledge. Poetry in particular thrived until about 1200 in the Moslem world, as it did not in the Christian world, and for a time, so too did philosophy. In medical science medieval Moslems were the leaders of the world. Many Moslem scholars simply assumed that human knowledge would, if properly employed, strengthen divine knowledge. But not all leaders of Moslem orthodoxy were so sure. An example of the problem is suggested by one of the great scholarly labors of the Middle Ages, undertaken by a secret fraternity of Moslem scientists and philosophers known as the "Brothers of Sincerity," who summarized Moslem thought in 51 treatises assembled in the year 983. This work was augmented by the greatest thinker of the early Moslem world, Avicenna, who, like many an intellectual before him, sought to reconcile philosophy with religion; and like many an intellectual after him, he drew heavily from Aristotle. But as time went on, suspicion of mere human efforts to capture truth increased. Powerful Moslem theologians found the speculations of Avicenna to be too daring and the works of the "Brothers of Sincerity" to be riddled with heresy. They not only feared the threat of speculative thought to the authority of the Koran, but they were convinced that the Koran itself contained quite enough knowledge for any Moslem. In 1150 the Caliph of Baghdad ordered all the works of Avicenna and the "Bretheren of Sincerity" to be burned, and so Arabic philosophy by the middle of the 12th century was effectively shut off in the East.

Meanwhile in the West, the works of Averroës, who was another great Moslem philosopher and who seemed even more enamored of Aristotle than of the

Koran, were also ordered to be burned in Seville in 1194. Thereafter Moslem thought lapsed back into blind orthodoxy, so that by the beginning of the 13th century the great intellectual history of the Moslem world, which at one time had excelled in science, medicine, mathematics, dialectics, and philosophy came to an end, and Islam as a world power began its long descent. The Moslem religion, however, went on and on and is still going on, perhaps because the speculations of Moslem intellectuals did not go on.

The fate of the intellectuals in the Jewish world in the Middle Ages also makes the Christian world look good. For a time, especially in the 12th century, Hebrew culture was second only to Moslem culture in its richness and variety, particularly in Spain. But medieval Jewish intellectuals were as naïve as Moslem intellectuals in setting out to demonstrate that man's reason would inevitably strengthen God's revelation. Their religion came from the Old Testament and especially the Talmud, and their philosophy came largely from Moslem thought.

Medieval Jewish thought culminated in the work of Maimonides, the most learned scholar in 12th century Europe, excepting perhaps Averroës. Maimonides made a supreme effort to reconcile Jewish thought with Judaism just as Averroës tried to reconcile Moslem thought with Mohammedanism, and he appeared to have succeeded so well that the whole learned world took cognizance of his works. Once again it seemed that a great thinker of the Western world had shown that God and man see eye to eye on the things that matter most. But just as the emirs and caliphs of Moslem orthodoxy concluded that Avicenna and Averroës did more to threaten Mohammedanism than to foster it in their attempt to rationalize religion, so the Talmudic rabbis concluded that Maimonides had done more to weaken

Judaism than to strengthen it. Rabbi Solomon ben Abraham of the University of Montpelier therefore not only anathematized the works of Maimonides but ordered the excommunication of all Jews who pursued profane learning or who made free with allegorical interpretations of the Scriptures. (He even explained to the Dominican Inquisition of Montpelier that Maimonides' books threatened Christianity, a revelation which led to a burning of them in Montpelier in 1234 and Paris in 1242, and the Talmud was also burned at Paris for good measure.) The followers of Maimonides responded at least to the extent of cutting out the tongues of Solomon's henchmen, and evidently killed Solomon too. But the medieval Jewish era of experimenting with a mixture of sacred and profane learning came to an end, and Judaism thereafter took refuge in fideism, mysticism, and isolation.

By contrast, the Christian church permitted a remarkable accumulation and dissemination of human learning. It is true that it did not do much to create a climate of free inquiry, but it showed its teeth only where the intellectuals showed theirs. Abelard, who was among the most important 12th-century intellectuals, also attempted to reconcile pagan philosophy and Christian doctrine and in the process showed his teeth. More than any Christian philosopher before him, he forced theology into the procrustean bed of reason and ruthlessly lopped off the parts that didn't fit. He also taught dozens of his disciples to do the same. To say the least, he made many a churchman nervous about his relentless application of reason to the orthodox positions on such doctrines as sin and Hell and free will and the omnipotence of God. His attempt to demystify Christian doctrine seemed in the minds of many churchmen to threaten the very authority of the Church, so that it is little wonder that the Church dragged out that hound of heaven, the great St. Bernard, to sniff out Abelard's heretical thoughts. In due time sixteen of his boldest propositions were condemned, and once he was even humiliated by being forced to burn his own book by his own hands. Ultimately he himself was silenced and sentenced to the monastery at Cluny. He died at the priory of St. Marcel after a period of abject piety, and his ashes ended up in Paris alongside those of his beloved Héloise.

Despite the fact that Abelard stepped on a good many theological toes, his works became so influential that he opened the speculative door to a great many scholastic philosophers who followed, and no one knew where the unwieldy battering ram of philosophy would strike the theological edifice next. Actually, the influence of Aristotle's thought upon philosophical speculation in the medieval world, not only among Mohammedan and Jewish intellectuals but Christian intellectuals as well, was so great and the threat to Christian doctrine so real, that in 1255 the University of Paris prohibited the study of all Aristotle's major works.

It is little wonder, then, that the golden age of heresy in medieval Europe occurred in the late 12th and 13th centuries. Bertold von Regensburg counted up 150 heretical sects in the 13th century. Some were harmless enough, but others, such as the Waldensians and the Albigensians, seemed to threaten the very existence of the Church. As a result, the Church began to play rough with its heretics. During the early centuries of Christianity in the West, the punishment was usually not more than excommunication, as Pope Leo IX had decreed. But as challenges to the teaching and authority of the Church stepped up as a result of a climate of increased speculation, so too did the penalties. In time the sentence of excommunication was advanced to banishment or imprisonment by the state, and, finally, in the 13th century, death—though it should be pointed out that the people were often more zealous in persecuting heretics than was the Church, and often held private burnings of the victims before the Church could get to them. In fact, the Church seems to have been goaded into more severe measures against heretics by the urgings of the upper classes.

The Waldensian heresy reflects well enough the tightening up of the Church's policy toward heretics. It was created by Peter Waldo, an unlearned businessman from Lyon. His lack of education, however, did not prevent him from using his intellect, and his intellect told him that he should give away all his riches to the poor and follow Christ, and in the process to preach to others to do the same, using only the literal interpretations, as opposed to the exegetical encrustations which Christian theologians had been accumulating over the centuries. Basically he was doing what St. Francis of Assisi was going to do a generation later, but he appears not to have done it right, for Francis ended up a saint, whereas Waldo ended up a heretic. Waldo produced a band of lay preachers, often as unlearned as he, who did the work of the Church without the Church's permission. The Church showed its contempt for their contempt of the world by excommunicating them one and all. But still their numbers increased and thereby forced the Church into sterner measures, including extermination. The slaughter of the Waldensians became one of the less savory chapters in the history of Christendom.

If the Waldensians constituted the leading anti-intellectual heresy of the time, the Albigensians constituted the leading intellectual heresy of the time. The Albigensians were also known as the Cathars and also as the Neo-Manicheans. Indeed their movement resurrected the chief teachings of Mani, who was Persian and not Christian, but who managed to wreak havoc among the Christians during the early centuries of Christianity because of the appeal of his teachings, which included the idea that God is good and matter is evil and that therefore God did not create matter. The Church at first took a tolerant view of their unorthodoxy and merely engaged them in debate; but as the seriousness of the threat became clearer, it took sterner measures to the point of organizing crusades against the offenders. A series of bloody wars ensued which lasted thirty years, and ended with the triumph of the Church and the wholesale slaughter of the Albigensians, as well as the destruction of much of southern France.

One might suppose that such fates as the Waldensians and Albigensians experienced would chasten those who were inclined to deviate from orthodoxy, but the fact is that heresies continued to spread faster and wider than the persecutions, so that the Church at last was forced to set up a systematic means of dealing with the threat of wayward intellectuals and their followers, namely the Inquisition, which was agreed to by both Church and state on the grounds that heresy is in fact treason. This agreement gave the state ultimate authority over the fate of the heretics.

The activities of the Inquisition, which was founded in 1230-33 by Pope Gregory IX, suggest that as the Church gained power it became increasingly impatient with its intellectual adversaries. In time, burning became the official method of handling heretics who seemed to threaten orthodoxy. Torture, too, was sometimes part of the treatment, and was not confined to intellectuals, but included even women and children, though pregnant women were ordered not to be tortured until their babies were born. It is easy, of course, to exaggerate both the severity of the punishment and number of the victims of the Inquisition. Nonetheless the phenomenon of the Inquisition suggests that the Church was by now quite willing to take the lives of men in order, as it thought, to preserve its own life.

But the point to be made here about these historic instances of heresy is that the heretics were not atheists nor barbarians, but Christians, and Christians of the most devout sort. They were all convinced that God had indeed spoken through the Sacred Scriptures; they did not doubt that Christ was God, and most of them subscribed to most of the fundamental doctrines of the Church. Many were quite as learned, and most were quite as believing Christians as the most powerful orthodox Christian intellectuals. Their problem was that they wanted human reason and human understanding to prevail, whereas the Church wanted its understanding or God's understanding to prevail. The age of the atheist intellectual was not yet. In fact, as the next chapter will suggest, it did not begin in earnest even during the Renaissance. Indeed, the heyday of the Christian intellectual was yet to come, in the form of Christian humanism.

CHAPTER III

THE PHENOMENON OF CHRISTIAN HUMANISM

Despite the efforts of intellectuals during the first fourteen centuries of Christianity to harmonize Christian doctrine and secular learning, the attitude of the official Church was that it couldn't be done. The contribution of the Christian humanists during the Renaissance was to show that it could be done, indeed that it was being done. There can be no doubt as to what the official position of the Church was before the advent of the Renaissance. It distrusted all the human faculties as reliable ways of arriving at the ultimate truths. It distrusted reason; it distrusted the imagination; it distrusted the memory; and it distrusted the senses.

It is necessary to have some understanding of the nature and extent of this distrust in order to appreciate what the Christian humanists accomplished. For Christian humanism, as I shall define it, means the belief that the basic *human* faculties, represented especially by reason, memory, and the imagination can all be handmaidens of religion; rather than lead to the destruction of Christianity, they can, properly used, fortify it. The study of philosophy and history and poetry, they held, is not only permissible, it is highly desirable. They therefore called for the study of the Greek and Latin languages because they recognized that the best philosophy and history and poetry were written in those languages. As Thomas More, one of the great Christian humanists in England, put it, "As to the question of humanistic education being secular, no one has ever claimed that a man needed Greek and Latin, or indeed any education in order to be saved. Still this education which is called secular does train the soul in virtue." They believed, as Sir Philip Sidney expressed it, that "the end of all learning is virtuous action." And the emphasis upon virtuous action arose from the recognition that it led to salvation, which in the Christian view is the goal of man.

They perceived that the earthly disciplines that best led to virtuous action were philosophy, literature, and history, which are properly identified as the humanities because they engage the highest human faculties. Science did not stand so high in the Christian humanist hierarchy because it was less obviously a major force in leading to virtuous action, and so they tended to downgrade it along with music, arithmetic, geometry, and astronomy, which made up the medieval quadrivium. The scientist, Sidney observed, "might be blind in himself"; the mathematician might "draw forth a straight line with a crooked heart," and the astronomer "looking to the stars might fall into a ditch."

The attitude of the Church softened toward the method of reason (philosophy) as a means to truth before it did toward literature and science. As we have seen, most of the efforts of Christian intellectuals to reconcile philosophy, including Greek and Roman philosophy, did not satisfy orthodox theologians, just as those of Jewish and Mohammedan intellectuals did not satisfy the demands of Jewish and Mohammedan orthodoxy: in fact, it sometimes led to excommunication or even burning. But during the centuries in which scholasticism prevailed, particularly under the aegis of Thomas

Aquinas, the Great Synthesis seemed at last to have been achieved, though there were still abundant instances where the reasoners' reason was found to threaten Revelation and religion. As we have seen, the age of Thomas Aquinas was the golden age of heresy. But still, by the 14th century the Church sanctioned scholastic thought while still keeping an eye on the scholastics, so that the Christian humanists did not have to fight so hard for philosophy as they did for poetry and history.

The Church's attitude toward poetry and the works of the imagination generally had been more consistently hostile even to the end of the Middle Ages. The medieval Church had caught the spirit of St. Augustine in its view of imaginative literature, and Augustine in turn had caught the spirit of Plato, who would not permit poets in his ideal Republic on the grounds that poetry "feeds and waters the passions rather than drying them up; she lets them rule, although they ought to be controlled, if mankind are ever to increase in happiness and virtue." Works of the imagination generally, whether they appealed to the eye or the ear or merely to the mind, were almost universally regarded as morally corrupting, though it is true that just as Plato permitted hymns of praise to the gods and to famous men, the Church in time permitted songs and paintings and sculptures which redounded to the glory of God and the saints. Christian hymns replaced pagan love songs, just as naked athletes were replaced by draped monks and Venuses by Marys.

But despite the fact that a few enlightened Fathers of the early Church tolerated or even advocated the study of poetry, the medieval Church did not encourage it. It was widely regarded as a waste of time, full of lies, and morally corrupting. Even the great cosmopolitan scholar Alcuin, the teacher of Charlemagne and spreader of classical learning, though steeped in pagan poetry himself, in later life came out against teaching it to Christian youths.

Religious opposition to the drama had a particularly long and distinguished history. The theater in the early Christian era was anathema to religious interests not only because of its pagan origins but because it appealed to the sensuality of both the eyes and the ears, as well as the mind: many of the early Church Fathers were glad to point this out. Tertullian devoted a whole treatise entitled *De Spectaculis* attacking pagan theatricals, which by that time were pretty immoral even by modern standards. Salvian, Cyprian, Chrysostom, and indeed most of the other Fathers of the Church also had something to say against them, until finally by an edict at the Council of Trullo in 692 theatrical activity finally came to an end.

It is one of the great ironies of cultural history that theatrical activity should once again grow out of religious ritual, not this time the ritual of the ancient Greeks but the Christian Mass. Tropes evolved into liturgical plays, which in turn developed into mystery and morality plays and finally turned into the full-blown secular plays of the late 16th century. When they reached that point they once again came under the guns of the clergy, particularly the Protestants in England. Concerted opposition of clergymen to the theater in fact did not die down until the 18th century when the plays got artistically worse and the Church got politically weaker.

Nor did the Church do much to encourage the study of history in any of the centuries before the Renaissance. Study of the past was simply not regarded as a fruitful way of arriving at truth, and often the Church was more interested in forgetting the past than recording it. The work of the great Greek historians, like Herodotus and Thucydides, had been lost or forgotten, and such history as was produced rarely rose above the primitive chronicle, or else was interpreted as the workings of Divine Providence rather than the result of the interaction between men and men.

Science and medicine fared little better. The main problem was that Christian traditions and doctrines prevented inquiry into the workings of the natural world, which was commonly regarded as the Devil's domain. Furthermore, the senses were supposed to have been dimmed by the Fall, so that whatever truths they could discern were automatically suspect. Actually, science in general and medicine in particular had already begun to deteriorate in the classical world before the Christians took over. But it is fair to inquire why, after the barbarian invasions ended, it did not resume its advance. One cannot help speculating that medicine fared badly in the medieval world because the main aim was the salvation of the soul, not the health of the body and that therefore the body would not get the attention of the best minds. On the other hand, as the soul and its salvation became less important in the modern world even to the point of being denied, there is a certain logic to the supposition that more and better minds would inquire into the nature of the body, and the caring of its ills. By that token the greatest medical advances ought to come in the period of greatest unbelief, namely the 19th and 20th centuries, and such indeed seems to have been the case. The medieval Church, on the other hand, discouraged surgery and prohibited dissection of corpses for the edification of doctors and medical students out of deference to the dignity of the human body. At any rate, the attitude of the Christian Church toward science must have had something to do with the fact that the discovery that the blood circulates through the body, a discovery which provided the foundation of modern medicine, had to wait until the 17th century.

All this is not to say that there was no poetry, no history, or no philosophy produced during the Middle Ages. Actually a good deal was produced, just as scientific investigation of sorts was also carried on, more in fact than one might expect under the circumstances. But it is to say that Christianity, as it was interpreted by the great theologians of the Church, especially in the fideistic spirit of St. Augustine, did not create a climate in which intellectual inquiry and imaginative creativity could flourish. As we have seen, however, intellectual inquiry did begin to come to life again in the 12th century and was greatly stepped up in the 13th century as the medieval universities took the intellectual lead.

In part this growth of secular learning came as a result of Aristotelian thought to some degree replacing Platonic thought. Plato, with his emphasis upon perfecting the human soul had tended to disparage the body, including especially the imagination and the senses, which he totally mistrusted and which, as we have seen, Christianity, particularly in Augustinian thought, also mistrusted. Aristotle, on the other hand, because he assigned a higher value to human faculties such as the memory, the imagination, and the senses, helped prepare the way for an epistemological acceptance not only of philosophy but also of poetry, science, and history as sources of truth.

In that sense the Christian humanists perpetuated the spirit of Aristotle and denigrated the spirit of Plato. Many Christian humanists, it is true, found much of Plato's thought to be wholly congenial and some of them undertook to revive him and to dethrone Aristotle, even to the point of establishing neo-Platonic academies. Similarly, Christian humanists in general tended to disparage scholastic philosophy, which was supported by Aristotelian thought. Basically, however, they were more nearly in agreement with Aristotle on the value of the human faculties than with Plato.

The Christian humanists' assertion that poetry and history as well as philosophy were handmaidens of religion was already being made in the first half of the 14th century, but the rediscovery of vast numbers of classical Greek and Latin manuscripts in the 14th and 15th centuries touched off the Renaissance, and the golden age of the Christian intellectual was at hand.

The story of the recovery of these manuscripts is one of the most astonishing developments in the cultural history of Western civilization. The most dramatic finds were those by Giovanni Aurispa, who from his travels in Greece brought back 238 manuscripts including the plays of Aeschylus and Sophocles, and by Francesco Filelfo, who in 1427 rescued from Constantinople texts of Herodotus, Thucydides, Polybius, Demosthenes, Aeschylus, Aristotle, and seven plays of Euripides. But other Italian scholars also made spectacular finds; the combined efforts of Poggio, Salutati, Landrini, and others recovered manuscripts of the works of Lucretius, Vitruvius, Plautus, Petronius, Cicero, Tacitus, Pliny the Younger, and a host of other writers, unknown or little known to the civilized world. Collecting ancient manuscripts, which now seemed to turn up everywhere, became a passion. The resulting excitement was sometimes almost too much to bear: Niccolo de Niccoli, a wealthy man, went broke buying them up, and one of the humanists, Andreoli de Ochis, was reported ready to sacrifice his home, his wife, and his life to add classical manuscripts to his library.

The Italian humanists set to work to peruse, to edit, to collate, to annotate, and to translate these manuscripts and above all to discuss them and to think about what it all meant. The chief question here is what the discovery of this newly found display of verbal brilliance did to their thinking about the answers to the eternal questions. Did they become pagans by studying the highest achievements of pagan minds? The question needs to be stressed because of the still common image of the Renaissance as a period in which men broke their religious fetters, asserted their independence from God and the Scriptures and, after the fashion of the classical writers, put their ultimate trust in reason. Jakob Burkhardt in his monumental work on the *Civilization of the Renaissance in Italy* (1863) was the original perpetrator of this view, and it is still fairly common. Burkhardt believed that the Italian humanists widely abandoned Christianity and the authority of the Scriptures in favor of the authority of the best minds of ancient Greece and Rome. "This humanism," he asserted, "was in fact pagan, and became more and more so as its sphere widened in the 15th century." Burkhardt's interpretation, however, is not any longer the dominant one, for more and more scholars have come to recognize that the Renaissance is far more nearly an extension of the medieval world than the beginning of the modern world. Christian doctrine, they now understand, was still at the core of the thinking of Renaissance intellectuals not only in Northern Europe, where it was in fact overwhelmingly so, but even in Italy, where undoubtedly the attractions of Roman and Greek pagan writers were most strongly felt. Douglas Bush in his study of *The Renaissance and English Humanism* offers the best summary of the best scholarship on the subject: "To put the matter briefly and somewhat too bluntly," he observed, "in the Renaissance the ancient pagan tradition (which does not mean neo-paganism), with all its added power, did not overthrow the medieval Christian tradition; it was rather, in the same way if not quite to the same degree as in the Middle Ages, absorbed by the Christian tradition."

Essentially, the Renaissance intellectuals wanted to adapt classical ideas to the Christian view of the world, which, as we have seen, is what some medieval intellectuals wanted to do also, but now there were more classical ideas more powerfully expressed; and so, many Christian humanists were more powerfully influenced by them. Some Renaissance theologians, it is true, accused the humanists of leaning too far toward paganism, but the humanists in turn cited the example of the early Church Fathers, who in varying degrees had used classical literature to support Christian doctrine. The fact that some Italian humanists seem to have been little concerned with Christianity and pursued their study of the classics without attempting to use them to strengthen Christian doctrine did not make them atheists. Even Burkhardt himself does not claim that the Italian humanists openly professed atheism. The humanists, he observed, "easily got the name of atheists, if they showed themselves indifferent to religion, and spoke freely against the Church, but not one of them ever professed, or dared to profess, a formal, philosophical atheism."

A few illustrations of the religious position of some of the most important Italian humanists will perhaps suggest how Christian they remained, despite their love of the pagan classics. The first Italian humanist was Petrarch (1304-74), and he did more perhaps than any other Renaissance figure to stimulate enthusiasm for classical learning. Although he took minor orders chiefly to fend off poverty, his basic orientation remained Christian. It is simply that his Christianity did not prevent him from losing himself in the world of the pagan classics. But he also studied the early Church Fathers, and if he quoted pagan authors more frequently than Christian authors in defense of Christianity, this practice merely suggests how compatible he found them to be with Christian doctrine. This is not to say, however, that Petrarch was wholly comfortable in his love for both Christ and Cicero. He in fact suffered many of the same doubts as Jerome and Augustine that the Christian mind and the classical mind could be truly reconciled, as his imaginary dialogue between himself and St. Augustine entitled *Secrets* suggests. In his essay *On His Own Ignorance*, furthermore, he defends being a virtuous man over being a learned man. Above all he wanted the study of the classics to make better Christians.

His confrere Giovanni Boccaccio (1314-75) was in the end at least as much a Christian as Petrarch. At about age 50, Boccaccio underwent a spiritual crisis and intended to become a monk, but Petrarch dissuaded him and urged him instead to continue his pursuit of classical learning; whereupon instead of joining a religious order, he plunged into a systematic study of the classics, even learning Greek, which Petrarch did not learn. His early life was about as secular as the stories in his *Decameron*, but he became thoroughly Christianized after his spiritual crisis and composed his works on *The Fall of Famous Men, The Fall of Famous Women*, and his *Genealogy of the Gods* with a full acceptance of Christian doctrine.

Others of the chief intellectuals of the Italian Renaissance were not less Christian than Petrarch and Boccaccio and many were more so. Marsilio Ficino, for example, founded the Platonic Academy of Florence, and for a time he gave up Christ for Plato and even burned candles before Plato's bust. But he got through a critical illness with the help of Augustine's works and so was won back to Christianity. For the last 24 years of his life he was a priest and evidently a good one. He wrote his *Theologica Platonica* specifically to try to reconcile Platonism and Christianity.

Pico della Mirandola, another of the great Italian humanists, was a member of Ficino's Platonic Academy, and one of its most learned members, having added Hebrew and Arabic to his Greek and Latin repertoire. Something of a prodigy, he published a list of 900 propositions on a wide variety of subjects; and since only three were condemned as heretical, he escaped ecclesiastical harrassment. Ficino, however, seems not to have been so comfortable with the combination of his learning and his Christianity, and in the end he more or less gave up the one for the other. Before he died at the age of 31 he became a follower of the religious reformer Savonarola, burned all his love poetry, designated that his wealth be turned into marriage dowries for indigent brides, and adopted a rigorously ascetic life—not out of love of Plato but of Christ. During his last years he concluded that only the Bible could satisfy his appetite for truth and he turned more and more to biblical study and began an elaborate apology for Christianity which his early death prevented him from completing.

Others of the most famous learned men of the Italian Renaissance were perhaps even more devout Christians, including, for example, Ambrogio Traversari, who died in 1438. As General of the Carmelite Order, he was one of the relatively few Italian scholars who interested himself in the Christian classics, and he translated the Greek Fathers into Latin. Gianozzo Manetti (1396-1459) was of a deeply religious turn of mind, a pioneer in the study of Hebrew, a translator of Aristotle's *Nichomachean Ethics*; among other works he wrote a treatise on the *Dignity and Excellence of Man*, as well as studies of Dante, Petrarch, and Boccaccio. Leonardo Bruni (1370-1444) was another devout Christian scholar, who became Chancellor of Florence. His *Latin History of the Florentine People* was the first distinctively humanistic history, and he translated Plato, Aristotle, and Plutarch.

Others of the major Italian intellectuals of the Renaissance who were profoundly Christian include Vittorino da Feltre, Guarino da Verona and Flavio Biondo. Some, in addition to Ficino, were clerics, like Tommaso Campanella, who was a Dominican monk, and who wrote more than 80 works, though he was imprisoned for heresy and later fled to France. Pietro Bembo, the propounder of Platonic love, represented in Castiglione's *The Courtier*, was a cardinal, in addition to being a veritable literary dictator and spokesman for the Ciceronians.

Some Renaissance popes also did much to encourage classical learning, among them Nicholas V, who was himself an enthusiastic collector of classical manuscripts, and Pius II, who was both a scholar and a writer, and who produced poems, dialogues, letters, a novel, a history and even a geography which reputedly influenced Columbus. Pope Sixtus IV was also a lavish patron of classical learning, and his nephew Leo X was one of the most munificent of all Renaissance popes, to the point that under his reign the center of the Renaissance moved from Florence to Rome.

Literally dozens of other names might be added to this list of major Italian humanists in order to suggest that their orientation remained Christian. At the same time, it is just as easy to err by insisting that the study of classical learning did not touch the faith of many intellectuals of the Italian Renaissance. The rediscovery of vast numbers of pagan Greek and Latin manuscripts in the 14th and 15th centuries and the subsequent revitalization of interest in classical thought led some humanists to a glorification if not a deification of writers like Cicero and Virgil, and for those who knew Greek, Homer and Plato and Aristotle. The brilliance of classical thought and imagination made the literature of Christianity seem pale and ineffectual—even the writings of the early Church Fathers. For those humanists who admired superior rhetoric and the beauty of words, the influence of classical thought was particularly strong.

A few Italian humanists, it is true, seemed unashamedly pagan, like Aretino, for example, who lived the obscenities of his writings, though the point to be made about Aretino is that he was nearly unique among his intellectual peers in his paganism. Furthermore, despite the efforts of some scholars to link him with the real spirit of the Italian Renaissance, he was pretty much, as Douglas Bush says, "an insignificant scoundrel." Many scholars now believe that Lorenzo Valla, the great Italian Latin scholar, was really attempting to purify the Church rather than destroy it in his attacks on the temporal power of the papacy, on scholasticism and monasticism, and on the Vulgate Bible.

Paul Oskar Kristeller sums up what must now be the best judgment concerning the Italian humanists' view of Christianity:

> There were many humanists who were not concerned with religious or theological problems, and did not touch on them in their writings. Those who did, and they were important, never undertook a general critique of the religious tradition such as appeared in the eighteenth century. They usually praised the Bible and the Church Fathers as the Christian classics, and attacked scholastic theology as barren distortion of original Christian doctrine and piety. A few of them attacked the weaknesses they observed in the Church of their time, and especially in monasticism. When the humanists wrote about moral subjects, either they tried to combine and to harmonize ancient and Christian ideas in the manner of Erasmus, or they discussed moral topics on a purely classical and secular basis—without however indicating any hostility toward Christianity, but rather taking for granted the compatibility between the two, as was done by Alberti and many other Italian humanists.

In the North, in Germany, Holland, and England, the Christian humanists placed a heavier emphasis upon *Christian* as was also the case in Spain and France. Such humanists as Budé, Casaubon, and Joseph Scaliger in France; Camerarius, Nicholas of Cusa, Johann Reuchlin, and Rodolphus Agricola in Germany; Elio Nebrija, Juan Vives, and Juan de Valdés in Spain; George Buchanan in Scotland; Desiderius Erasmus and Hugo Grotius in Holland; and John Colet, Thomas Linacre, Thomas More, Sir Thomas Elyot and Roger Ascham in England are representative of Renaissance humanism outside Italy, and most of them were profoundly Christian. Some of them were so Christian in fact that they became embroiled in religious controversy defending this or that Christian position, and some of them, like Scaliger, Camerarius, Buchanan, Elyot, and Ascham, were Protestants, suggesting how far Protestant intellectuals also participated in Renaissance Christian humanism.

Erasmus was Holland's chief contribution to Christian humanism. He was an Augustinian monk but was given unrestricted freedom to travel so that his presence and influence permeated all Europe, and thus earned him the title "Prince of Humanists." A compulsive writer, he wanted to instruct everyone: he wrote Latin grammars and textbooks, for example, *Copiae Verborum* for schoolboys; handbooks for the aristocracy, such as his *Enchiridion Militis Christiani*; works for intellectuals, such as his best-seller *Familiar Colloquies*; and guides for Christian leaders, such as his *Education of a Christian Prince*. For the clergy he wrote his *Ecclesiastes*, showing them how to preach, and for theologians he edited a new Greek edition of the New Testament. For Protestants he wrote defenses of Catholicism, and for nearly everyone he wrote his most famous work, *In Praise of Folly*. But as a relentless Christian humanist he always aimed to combine "good letters" with "the philosophy of Christ."

Guillame Budé, who was among the giants of French Renaissance intellectuals, undertook to establish the relationship between Hellenism and Christianity in his treatise *Transitus*, and Isaac Casaubon was a theologian as well as a classical scholar who later settled in England and joined the Church of England. Elio Antonio de Nebrija was Spain's first humanist, and his chief interest was biblical exegesis. The Protestant Juan de Valdés was frightened by the Inquisition because of his unorthodox theological views, particularly as expressed in his *Dialogue of Christian Doctrine*, and so settled in Naples where he gathered a group of pious and learned friends about him. Johann Reuchlin, the greatest of the German humanists and a strong advocate of the study of Hebrew as a means to understanding the Old Testament, was accused by the Inquisition but defended by most of the humanists of Europe and finally acquitted by Pope Leo X.

But perhaps nowhere were piety and learning more harmoniously combined than in the Christian humanists of Renaissance England. The spirit of Christian humanism in 16th-century England was established by a small circle of scholars that included William Grocyn, Thomas Linacre, John Colet, and Thomas More. All of them except More had studied in Italy and returned fired with enthusiasm for classical learning, which they sought to spread throughout the land in a pronounced Christian context. Grocyn was a priest and was called even in his own time "the patriarch of English learning." After studying in Florence and Rome he returned to England to teach Greek at Oxford, numbering Thomas More and Erasmus among his students. Erasmus described him as "a man of the most severe and chaste life, exceedingly observant of ecclesiastical rules, almost to the point of superstition, and to the highest degree learned in scholastic theology; while he was, at the same time, a man gifted by nature with the most acute judgment and exactly versed in every description of educational knowledge." Thus Grocyn seemed to epitomize the Christian humanist ideal in his combination of piety and learning.

Thomas Linacre, who received his medical degree from the University of Padua, was particularly interested in science and medicine. He translated Galen into Latin, founded the London College of Physicians, compiled a Latin grammar and taught Greek at Oxford, none of which activities appear to have diminished his Christian piety. John Colet, who was perhaps more Christian than humanist, returned from Italy to lecture on the Epistles of St. Paul at Oxford, and to exhort the English clergy, including the bishops, to reform their lives. Thomas More, apart form being a martyr and a saint as well as Lord Chancellor of England, was exceedingly learned in Latin and Greek. In spite of his political career, which consumed most of his time, he never lost his interest in classical learning, and he wrote a moving and forceful letter to the dons of Oxford exposing the so-called Trojans among them, who "think Greek is a joke for the simple reason that they don't know what good literature is." "To these modern 'Trojans'," he warns, "applies the old saw, 'Trojans always learn too late'." More's religious activity included verbal embroilments in religious controversy, chiefly against the Protestants. While these do not reflect what Erasmus called his "gentle, sweet, and happy" nature, they do reflect the depth of his religious conviction.

These men, together with Erasmus, were known as the Oxford Reformers, and they were indeed reformers, not only spiritual but academic reformers. They agitated both for more Christianity and for more humanism. The greatest legacy of the Renaissance Christian humanists came from their educational theories and practices, with a new emphasis upon literature and history and rhetoric, with a corresponding de-emphasis upon the medieval quadrivium—arithmetic, geometry, astronomy, and music. Most of them were professors, teachers, writers of textbooks, founders of schools and academies, or in one way or another connected with education. But one and all they proceeded on the premise that the chief value of education was to make better Christians.

Johannes Sturm, the German humanist and headmaster of Strassburg Gymnasium for 43 years, was the most influential schoolmaster not only in Germany but probably in the entire European continent. His school became the model Latin grammar school for all of Germany, and in his chief work he defined his Christian ideal of education, supplementing it with a series of Latin graded readers used to prepare students to read the best of the Latin classics. Similarly, Vittorino da Feltre was the most famous schoolmaster of Renaissance Italy. He founded a boarding school on the study of the classics but with the aim of preparing students for lives of moral virtue and cultivated leisure. His school became a Christian nursery of humanism and a model for similar schools all over Italy. And Erasmus, the greatest of them all, was an educator before everything else, a Christian educator dedicated to educating Christians.

And yet it was in England that theories of Christian humanistic education were brought to the fullest perfection. Perhaps the single most important event in the history of Christian humanist education in England was the founding by John Colet of St. Paul's School in 1512. It is important because St. Paul's became the model for

Latin grammar schools which in time were to be established all over England. They were to produce most of England's great poets, dramatists, philosophers, and scholars, and were to enable England to lead the Western world not only in humane letters but in Christian humane letters. A few lines from Colet's "Statutes of Paul's School" will suggest what he had in mind:

> I would there were taught always the good literature, both Latin and Greek, and good authors such as have the very Roman eloquence joined with wisdom, especially Christian authors that wrote their wisdom with clean and chaste Latin, either in verse or in prose; for my intent is by this school especially to increase knowledge and worshipping of God and our Lord Christ Jesus and good Christian life and manners in the children.

Colet provided the money and wisdom to found the school, Erasmus provided the textbooks, and William Lyly, another Christian humanist, became the first headmaster and provided the academic and spiritual guidance. Shakespeare, Spenser, Milton, and most of the great poets and dramatists of Renaissance England came from Christian humanist schools which had been modelled on St. Paul's.

Later Christian humanists in England perpetuated the recognition that classical learning can lead to "virtuous action," and hence, to salvation through Christ. Sir Thomas Elyot, for example, in his *Boke Named the Governour*, emphasized the study of classical literature because of the contribution it could make to the moral development of the Christian governors of Christian commonwealths; and in the process, he demonstrated how far Protestantism participated in the spirit of Christian humanism. He called for the study of the Greek and Latin languages between the ages of 7 and 13, for the study of Aesop, Lucian ("though it were better that a child should never read any part of Lucian than all of Lucian"), Aristophanes, Homer, Virgil, Ovid, Silius Italicus, Lucan, Hesiod, and so on. From ages 14 to 17 the student should learn logic, rhetoric, history, and cosmography; and after 17 philosophy and theology. In his emphasis upon the moral purpose of learning, Elyot reflects the educational ideal of the best Christian humanist tradition.

So too did Roger Ascham, another learned Protestant and tutor to Queen Elizabeth, in his renowned *Schoolmaster*. "Learning," he insisted, "and good bringing up, and not blind and dangerous experience, is the next and readiest way that must lead your children first to wisdom and then to worthiness," i.e., to moral excellence. Ascham was, however, nearly unique in England in his command of Greek and hence in his emphasis upon Greek over Latin, Italian, Spanish, French, and Dutch literature. "Cicero only excepted," he says, "and one or two more in Latin, they be all patched clouts and rags in comparison of fair woven broadcloths; and truly if there be any good in them, it is either learned, borrowed, or stolen from some one of those worthy wits of Athens."

Thus Ascham recommends the best of the Greek writers in training the three basic human faculties, reason, memory, and the imagination, as instruments of moral excellence, not for its own sake, but for God's sake. He is quite as conscientious as Elyot in warning students away from literature that can have a corrupting influence. The Arthurian legends, he insists, lead "to none other end than manslaughter and bawdry." The feeling of moral superiority among northern Protestants over Italian Catholics is reflected in Ascham's disapproval of the widespread practice of English students' studying in Italy. "The Italianate Englishman," he reminds them, "is the Devil Incarnate." Furthermore, "ten Morte

Arthurs do not a tenth part so much harm as one of these books made in Italy and translated in England."

Testimonies to the belief that secular learning can lead to virtuous action can be found everywhere among the Christian humanists in Renaissance England, particularly imaginative literature, which, as we have seen, was pretty thoroughly discouraged in the Middle Ages. Poetry, says John Harrington, scholar and translator of *Orlando Furioso*, can "soften and polish the hard and rough disposition of men and make them capable of virtue and good discipline." Samuel Daniel in his *Musophilus* exalted the role of the poet to a level higher than at any time since the Golden Age of Greece:

> Thou that canst do much more with one poor pen
> Than all the powers of princes can effect,
> And draw, divert, dispose, and fashion men
> Better than force or rigor can direct.

Spenser wrote *The Faerie Queene* precisely in order to "fashion a gentleman or noble person in virtue and gentle discipline." And Milton, the last great Christian humanist of the Renaissance, was glad to point out that Spenser is "a better teacher than Scotus or Aquinas."

Sir Philip Sidney in his *Apology for Poetry* wrote what is undoubtedly a more persuasive defense of imaginative literature as a means to virtue than anyone else in Renaissance Europe. In the best display of rhetoric that had yet appeared in English, Sidney demonstrated that poetry more effectively leads men to virtuous action than even history or philosophy, which in typical Christian humanist fashion he regarded as the other two most important forms of secular learning.

And yet despite the apparent harmonizing of religious knowledge and secular knowledge by the Christian humanists, the Renaissance was quite as much an age of controversy as any other and quite as much an age of epistemological ferment. There were still plenty of churchmen who were not as willing as the Christian humanists to assign so high a place to the secular disciplines as a means to salvation. And although many Protestant clergymen were highly learned, some tended to perpetuate the medieval distrust of reason, imagination, and memory. Luther had himself declared that "Reason is the Devil's whore," and Puritan clergymen were often quite as suspicious of imaginative literature and the arts, especially the drama, as the Church of the early centuries of Christianity. In some ways Protestantism marked a return to fideism, to the spirit of Augustine and, before him, to Plato.

But apart from the bitter conflicts between the Catholics and the Protestants, there were also lively contests of all sorts in the intellectual arena of the Renaissance, between the Aristotelians and the Platonists, the nominalists and the realists, the scholastics and the anti-scholastics, the Ciceronians and the anti-Ciceronians, and so on and on. But the point here is that regardless of what position the intellectuals took in these controversies, they were virtually all conducted within the Christian pale. Heresy and the persecution of heretics still thrived, but the line between heresy and orthodoxy became increasingly unclear, and sometimes neither the Catholics nor the Protestants knew whom to burn. Nests of genuine atheists were not unknown, but when they were known they made news, as, for example, the School of Night in England, which boasted among its members such notables as Sir Walter Raleigh. The term atheist, however, was often rather loosely used to include many whose religious thought was free, even freewheeling, but who by modern standards might be regarded as bastions of orthodoxy. The anti-religious sentiments of Rabelais or the universal skepticism of Montaigne can in no way be taken as typical of Renaissance thought, any more than the unabashed paganism of a few Italian writers.

It is difficult to make many generalizations about so complex a period as the Renaissance without being challenged at every turn; but it does seem possible to conclude that the Renaissance did not provide a climate in which intellectuals who were true unbelievers could thrive. The overwhelming majority of intellectuals were still Christian, whether they were humanists or not. It was to be more than two centuries before intellectuals in chorus were to say "there is no God." But, immediately after the Renaissance, they began to hedge as to what kind of a God there is, and, as the next chapter will suggest, it less and less resembled the Christian God of the Middle Ages and the Renaissance.

CHAPTER IV

THE DE-CHRISTIANIZING OF THE INTELLECTUALS

In the 16th century most of the influential European intellectuals were, as we have seen, Christians, but by the end of the 18th century most of them were not, and have not been up to the present time either in Europe or America. The de-Christianizing of the intellectuals in the history of the Western world is of the utmost importance because it marks the abandonment of the belief that God spoke directly to men through the Scriptures in order to tell them how they should live and not live, and why. In place of the revealed God of Christianity, the most influential intellectuals adopted an unrevealed God in the 18th century, as this chapter will indicate, and then repudiated the whole idea of God in the 19th century, as the next chapter will indicate. In effect, what they did is to declare themselves willing to stand or fall on the belief that civilization can thrive on the unaided wisdom of men.

The de-Christianizing of the intellectuals meant the repudiation of the authority of the Scriptures as God's word by reducing them to mere philosophy and history and poetry like any other philosophy and history and poetry. It therefore meant also the repudiation of the authority of the Church, either Catholic or Portestant, because the Church depends upon the authority of the Scriptures. It meant also a denial of personal immortality with its attendant doctrines of Heaven and Hell. And above all it meant a repudiation of the doctrine of Original Sin, upon which most of the fundamental teachings of Christianity depended, including the Incarnation, the Redemption, and the Atonement, as well as the doctrines of Grace and Sin and the Sacraments.

It meant instead a greater confidence in the powers of reason than at any time since the age of the Greek and Roman philosophers. It meant an infinite faith in man himself either to find the final answers to the final questions or else to conclude that they cannot be found. It meant in fact pretty much what Burkhardt and his followers found in their study of the Italian Renaissance, except that it happened not in Italy in the 14th and 15th centuries as Burkhardt maintained, but in England and France and Germany in the 18th century. The de-Christianizing of the intellectuals meant, in what is perhaps the best definition of the term, the beginning of the modern world.

This de-Christianizing process was of course extremely complex and at first it proceeded slowly. The weakening of the authority of religion in 17th- and 18th-century Europe was the result of a wide variety of causes: social, political, economic, as well as intellectual causes which reach well back into the Rennaissance. The Babylonian Captivity (1305-77), the Great Western Schism (1378-1415), the increasingly serious quarrels between popes and princes, especially in England and France, the founding of national monarchies, the ever-increasing dissoluteness of the clergy and corruption in the Church, the horrible wars, both holy and unholy, and a host of other factors contributed immensely to weakening the authority of religion and the Church.

But it is the intellectual causes with which this study is properly concerned, and indeed it may well be that in the long run they are the most important. At the risk of gross over-simplification, I should like to identify three strains of Renaissance thought which became increasingly potent and which contributed most to the de-Christianizing of the intellectuals in the 18th century, namely (1) rationalism, (2) anti-rationalism, and (3) scientism, which exalt respectively the reason, the emotions, and the senses over Revelation.

1. Rationalism

The harmonious relationship between human knowledge and divine revelation which the Renaissance humanists appeared to have brought about was not to endure for long. The intellectual history of Christianity even to the end of the Middle Ages was a constant struggle between reason and revelation, between philosophy and faith; and orthodox Christian intellectuals had always been fearful that the authority of reason would in time undermine the authority of Revelation. As it turned out, their fears were well-founded, for although reason became the handmaiden of religion during the late Middle Ages, and even the wife during the Renaissance, it became the domineering matron during the later 17th and 18th centuries, and finally, the widow in the 19th.

All the while that the Renaissance Christian humanists were insisting upon the power of philosophy and poetry and history as instruments of virtue, and hence salvation, they were unwittingly undermining the very doctrines of Christianity upon which they built their arguments. For even though most Renaissance thought was bounded by fundamental Christian doctrine, there was a tendency to trust the human faculties more and more and to rely upon revealed truths less and less. A certain arrogance can be detected even among the leading 12th-century Christian intellectuals on this score in their attempt to bring religion down to the level of their own understanding. Abelard was a particularly notable example of this phenomenon, or at least St. Bernard thought so, and so were the Christian Averroïsts generally.

Furthermore, the Christian humanists did not have a corner on recommending virtue and good behavior, for classical writers had done so too, including Aristotle, Plato, Cicero, Plutarch, Seneca, Marcus Aurelius, and Epictetus. The Christian humanists were more or less thoroughly familiar with these writers and justly admired them, even venerated them inasmuch as they supported Christian principles. But this veneration opened the way for intellectuals to speculate that morality could be based upon philosophy quite as adequately as upon religion, that reason could provide adequate motives for good behavior without having to rely upon the fear of the just God of traditional Christianity and the admonitions of the Scriptures.

Such encroachments of rationalism upon religion in the 17th century are probably more readily demonstrable in England than in any other European country. By 1610 the burning of heretics came to an end in England, and the spirit of latitudinarianism began to take hold. Lord Herbert of Cherbury, who has been given the title of the "Father of English Deism," undertook to find the lowest common denominator of Christian belief in England, which, on account of the multiplication of Protestant sects over a period of a century, was then pretty low. In 1624 in his work *De Veritate* he laid down the chief principles of the deists' creed which were widely assumed by deists who followed, namely: (1) that there is one supreme God, (2) that He should be worshipped, (3) that virtue and piety are the chief parts of divine worship, (4) that men ought to be sorry for their sins and repent of them, and (5) that divine goodness dispenses rewards and punishments, both in this life and after it. Lord Herbert thought that all of these principles could be readily arrived at by reason alone. He did not repudiate Revelation outright, but he tended to treat the Scriptures as ordinary history and he ridiculed "bibliolatry."

Such then were the first tentative steps toward rationalizing Christianity. By the middle of the 18th century, however, most of the leading deists had repudiated all but the first of these principles, so that Samuel Johnson's definition of a deist in his *Dictionary* of 1755 as "a man who follows no particular religion but only acknowledges the existence of God, without any article of faith," seems quite accurate.

English intellectuals were not willing to follow Lord Herbert immediately in his de-emphasis of Revelation and his exaltation of reason as a means to religious truth, but John Locke, meanwhile, was contributing his bit by writing *The Reasonableness of Christianity*. At first glance this work might seem a latter-day effort to reconcile reason with Revelation after the fashion of the medieval philosophers, but in effect it constitutes a repudiation of virtually all the fundamental doctrines of Christianity in favor of mere human reasonableness, so that Abelard by comparison seems reactionary. In a sense, Locke was too Christian to be a deist and too much a deist to be a Christian. In his eagerness to gather everyone into the same Christian tent he reduced the fundamental Christian beliefs to two: "Faith and repentence," he wrote, "that is, believing Jesus to be the Messiah, and a good life, are the indispensable conditions of a new covenant to be performed by all those who obtain eternal life." Although Locke never doubted mankind's redemption by Christ, the infallibility of the Scriptures, or even the reality of miracles, he imbibed the latitudinarianism of the age, and he helped to pull the teeth of Christianity.

There is some justification for Santayana's observation that in Locke's basic philosophical position "his Christianity almost disappeared."

The fact is that Locke's sweet and warm reasonableness was so persuasive that he spawned a race of truly hardnosed rationalists both in England and on the Continent, who contributed immeasurably to the decline of the role of Christianity in the thinking of the most influential intellectuals to come. The rationalists, in fact, were making such headway that even by the end of the 17th-century Christianity had only its bare gums with which to defend itself. The deists in particular were pressing onward. Charles Blount, an acknowledged disciple of Lord Herbert, published his most outspoken work entitled *Summary Account of the Deist's Religion* in 1693, a few months before his suicide, in which he reiterated the rationalist approach to religion. John Toland, in his *Christianity not Mysterious* (1696) tried to rationalize the Scriptures and to throw out Christian mysteries because they were mysterious. Because of his prodigious learning and prolific writing, he did much to spread the spirit of deism around Europe. Similarly, Anthony Collins in his *Discourse of Free-Thinking* dignified free-thinking by calling the role of free-thinkers from the time of the ancient Greeks through Montaigne, Tillotson, and Locke.

A telling blow to the authority of the Scriptures in England was delivered by Matthew Tindal, who was the most learned of the British deists and the most important historically. His chief work, entitled *Christianity as Old as the Creation: or, the Gospel: A Republication of the Religion of Nature*, was first published in 1736 and became recognized at once as "the deist's Bible." Tindal always maintained the title of "Christian deist," but in effect he largely reasoned Christianity out of existence. Having reviewed in detail the inconsistencies and contradictions of the Scriptures, he concluded that the Scriptures are not necessary to religion after all, and that in any case all men are capable of Right Reason, which must give them all the truths they need to conduct themselves in life.

By the middle of the 18th century, Tindal had plenty of support, and deists began to pop up everywhere in England, including William Wollaston, who attacked the miracles of Christ in a treatise which Voltaire said was the most daring attack on Christianity ever to appear; and the Viscount Bolingbroke, who, while professing a belief in an uninterested deist God, ridiculed the authority of the Bible. These and a host of other mid-18th-century thinkers reinforced the trend toward the authority of reason and away from Revelation as the ultimate source of truth. Christianity in England was now clearly under siege, and when the weapons of such writers as Gibbon and Hume were added to the conflict, it became increasingly clear that intellectuals who still subscribed to the fundamental doctrines of Christianity and the ultimate authority of Scripture did not represent the wave of the future.

The fact is, however, that, in general, British intellectuals of the 17th and 18th centuries were more gentle in their treatment of Christianity than the French. Beginning with Descartes, the break with Christianity in France was less ceremonious and more precipitous than in England. In effect, what Descartes did was to decontaminate reason. The truths of religion, he insisted, must be taken on faith, for they are not susceptible to the scrutiny of reason. This position must seem like a return to early medieval fideism, but acutally it is not, because Descartes placed more faith in his own raw reason than in God's Revelation. He tended to regard the truths of reason as more reliable, if not indeed more important than the truths of religion. He deduced the existence of God and of immortality not from the Bible but from the fact of his own existence.

In a sense, Descartes' chief contribution to intellectual history is that he showed the most influential minds of Europe how philosophy could operate wholly independently of religion, or at least of revealed religion. What he did was to isolate philosophy from theology and to declare that theology was not the province of reason. Thus, what Thomas Aquinas had joined together Descartes put asunder. If there was anything left of scholastic philosophy by the middle of the 17th century, Descartes administered to it the *coup de grâce*.

Descartes was not himself an atheist, but he assigned fewer powers to God than had any previous philosopher of the Christian era. Pascal seems to have plumbed the depths of Descartes' theology when he observed in his *Pensées* that "Descartes would have liked to do without God, but he could not avoid letting Him give a little push to set the world in motion. After that he was finished with God." And so the Age of Reason in France begins, and the Age of Faith begins to end.

The effects of rationalism upon religion in France were most dramatically felt among the 18th-century *philosophes*, who opposed Christianity in general and the French Catholic Church in particular. It so happened that they were among the most influential intellectuals in France and included, among others, Voltaire, Diderot, d'Alembert, Helvétius, and d'Holbach.

Whereas the English deists and the Church of England had carried on a relatively friendly quarrel over the authority of reason versus revelation, the war between the *philosophes* and the Catholic Church in France was bloody, and no quarter was given. The *philosophes* condemned the Church and its teachings, and the Church condemned the works which condemned it.

After the expulsion of the Huguenots, there was no Protestant buffer in France between the secular mind and the religious mind, so that the choice seemed to lie between absolute belief and virtual atheism.

The most influential intellectuals chose not to believe, and they took their inspiration from earlier rebels like Montaigne, Descartes, Gassendi, Bayle, and Montesquieu, who together had built up a respectable intellectual tradition of anti-religious thought, or who had at least allowed their reason to overrule their religion. At the same time the *philosophes* drew sustenance from the minds of English writers—Bacon, Newton, Hobbes, and Locke, not to mention the Jewish philosopher Spinoza from Holland.

Of the great *philosophes*, perhaps the one least unfriendly to religion was Voltaire, despite the fact that he spent much of his life attacking the Church. Even to the end of his days he professed to believe in God, and he died in the Catholic Church. However, throughout the last 15 years of his life, he not only rejected the fundamental doctrines of the Church, but launched an obsessive campaign against Christianity. Yet he cannot properly be called an atheist, and by his own insistence, not even a deist, but a theist, which he himself defined as "a man firmly persuaded of the existence of a Supreme Being, equally good and powerful, who has formed all existences; who punishes crimes without cruelty, and rewards virtuous action with kindness." Actually, Voltaire's true religious beliefs are very hard to identify because of his constant contradictions and a lurking suspicion of insincerity. But he can, on balance, be said to have disbelieved more than he believed, and to have done more to Christianity than for it.

Many of his fellow *philosophes*, however, were far less equivocal in their religious position. With less hesitancy as also with less reflection they reaffirmed their faith in their unaided reason and repudiated their faith in Christianity. While mid-18th-century England still regarded the deists as dangerously radical thinkers, the French intellectuals, though previously trailing the English in radical thinking, had already passed from deism to virtual atheism. After a brief flirtation with deism, Diderot, the leading French encyclopedist, concluded that deists had simply not done enough thinking to become atheists, for he himself had been a deist before he did some more thinking. He even developed a whole theory of materialism which left no place either for Christianity or for any other religious position. There is evidence to suggest, too, that Diderot drew d'Alembert, his fellow encyclopedist, from his own skeptical deist position into the more airy tent of atheist materialism. In a letter to a friend, Diderot makes crystal clear his position on Christianity:

> The Christian religion is to my mind the most absurd and atrocious in its dogmas; the most unintelligible, the most metaphysical, the most subject to divisions, sects, schisms, heresies; the most mischievous for the public tranquility, the most dangerous to sovereigns by its hierarchic order, its persecutions, its discipline; the most flat, the most dreary, the most Gothic and most gloomy in its ceremonies; the most puerile and unsociable in its morality; . . . the most intolerant of all.

And yet there were *philosophes* who were more thoroughly de-Christianized than Diderot. Julien La Mettrie had already, before Diderot, devised a materialistic philosophical system which insisted that man was merely a machine and that all of his behavior had physical causes. Man's soul, if he had a soul, was purely physical, and was therefore the province of the physician, not the theologian; and in his work entitled *L'Homme Machine* may be found one of the first outright expressions of atheism in France. In La Mettrie's view, the existence of God and the authority of the Church and the Scriptures have no meaning.

La Mettrie's materialism marked the farthest departure yet from Christianity among French philosophers; he met his equal in that respect in England perhaps only in Hobbes. And he had his influence among other *philosophes*, not only in Diderot's thinking, but in that most avid materialist and opponent of religion of them all in Enlightened France, namely the Baron d'Holbach. In some ways d'Holbach represents the ultimate in confidence in the powers of mere reason, but d'Holbach was not content merely to declare that man didn't need God; almost everything he wrote was in one way or another an attack upon religion in general, and Christianity in particular. And in addition, he gathered around him some of the most influential intellectuals in France, including not only Diderot and d'Alembert, but men like Melchior von Grimm, Claude Helvétius, Rousseau, Boulanger, Etienne Condillac, and Condorcet, all of whom were caught up in the spirit of deism, if not outright atheism and materialism. In France, by the third quarter of the 18th century, the Age of the Christian Intellectual had ended, just as it had ended in England, and with the advent of the German Romantics, as we shall see in the next chapter, it ended in Germany too.

2. Anti-rationalism

As important as rationalism was in the de-Christianizing of European intellectuals, it was in some ways less important than the anti-rationalism which ran concurrently with rationalism from the 16th century onward and which continued even after rationalism began to lose its hold toward the end of the 18th century.

At first the anti-rationalism among intellectuals during the Renaissance had the effect of strengthening religion, particularly the fideist tradition which, though it had lost much influence with the rise of scholasticism, never really died out even when Renaissance Christian humanism was at its height. The idea that the real truth is the revealed truth and that human learning by comparison is vain if not downright dangerous always had its adherents, not so much in its extreme form as represented by Tertullian in his declaration, "I believe because it is absurd," which emphasized the futility of the human intellect in arriving at the truth, but in the more moderate fideism of Augustine in his position that "I believe in order to understand," which admitted that reason could, at least to some degree, buttress faith. Fideism could take the form of mysticism, as it did, for example, with St. John of the Cross, inasmuch as it invites direct experience with God without the aid of a trained human mind. But much of the fideism of the late Middle Ages and the Renaissance was in the Augustinian tradition. Even the Christian humanists were appalled at the presumption of the scholastics in their attempts to place all relvelation within the pale of reason. Petrarch speaks contemptuously of those scholastics who discuss the mysteries of Christianity "as though they had come from Heaven, and had been in Almighty God's council." But the Christian humanists themselves were often charged with placing too much faith in what men know and not enough in what God knows. The German scholar Cornelius Agrippa, in his work *On the Vanity of Human Knowledge*, reminds them all with some sarcasm that "Christ teaches that perfect virtue is not to be had except by grace given from above, but the philosophers say that men get it by their own strength and exercise." And Montaigne in his *Apology of Raymond Sebond* wrote one of the most devastating of all Renaissance attacks upon the claims of human knowledge as a means to learning God's ways.

Such skepticism among Renaissance intellectuals was in fact rather widespread, but nowhere perhaps did it take hold so firmly as in the anti-rationalistic sentiments of Luther, whose attacks on reason were more nearly reminiscent of Tertullian than Augustine. Luther was acutely aware that reason and philosophy in the hands of St. Thomas and his scholastic successors might in time threaten the authority of religion and the Scriptures. "I shall chop off the head of philosophy," he declared. "One should learn philosophy only as one learns witchcraft, that is to destroy it." Aristotle is therefore "an urchin who must be put in the pigsty or donkey's stable."

As everyone knows, for a time the fideistic spirit of Lutheranism, together with the influence of Calvin, produced a religious zeal that Christianity had not known for hundreds of years, and seriously threatened even the very existence of the Catholic Church, which by then was badly in need of reform. But, in time, Luther's effect upon intellectuals led them away from religion not only because of his anti-intellectual stance, but also because of his doctrine of total depravity. At first glance the doctrine of total depravity might seem to have fortified religion because it made men more dependent than ever upon God for their salvation. Calvin made even more of the doctrine of total depravity than Luther by coupling it with the doctrine of predestination. Furthermore, this view of human nature was to receive powerful support from Hobbes in the middle of the 17th century, who, however, would not admit the saving grace of God.

But as it turned out, the concept of total depravity proved to be psychologically intolerable, for no one can endure very long the idea that he himself is totally depraved. A reaction was bound to set in. It was merely a matter of time before intellectuals found a way out of the dilemma, and their solution was to conclude that man is not only not depraved; he is in fact naturally good, totally good, and the best part of him is not his reason as the Christian humanists and the Enlighteners insisted but in fact his feelings. What counted was religious feeling, not religious reason. If man is totally good, then his emotions are totally good and they can be trusted as never before.

The whole tradition of mysticism in Christianity, as indeed in other religions, is predicated upon the inferiority of reason to emotion; but never before had emotion achieved such recognition as a way to truth as it did in reaction to the doctrine of the total depravity of man which Reformation leaders (as well as those under the very different influence of Hobbes), had insisted upon. But Christian mysticism is not the same thing as merely trusting one's own instincts as guides to morality. In Christian mysticism Christ is still the Guide; in natural religion, based upon the infallibility of feeling and instinct, such as in Rousseau's, man himself is the guide, and in fact Christ is no longer needed. Thus the doctrine of the total depravity of man led, by way of reaction, to the opposite doctrine of the natural goodness of man. There was a certain inevitability that Luther's and Calvin's low view of human nature should eventually lead to Shaftesbury's and Rousseau's high view of human nature, that pro-faith should lead to pro-feeling, and that both should be anti-rational.

The idea of the natural goodness of man and hence the divinity of his emotions did not come directly from the rationalists, though the emphasis by 17th- and 18th-century intellectuals upon the efficacy of reason tended to imply a kind of natural goodness, especially in the insistence of those deists who believed that men would be guided by Right Reason if only they knew what Right Reason was. The new faith in the natural goodness of man's feelings, as opposed to his reason, appears to be traceable to the latitudinarian clergymen of late 17th-century England. For some decades before Shaftesbury gave full philosophical expression to the idea of the natural goodness of man in his *Characteristics* (1711), English clergymen like Benjamin Whichcote, Samuel Parker, Bishop Tillotson, and Jeremy Collier were reacting to the idea of the total depravity of man by emphasizing men's feelings as proper guides to virtuous behavior. R. S. Crane, who has studied closely the sermons and treatises on moral philosophy of late 17th-century England, describes this extremely important development as follows:

> When Shaftesbury in 1698 praised Benjamin Whichcote for his defense of "Natural Goodness," he was using phrases which might have been applied, with little qualification, to most of the leading divines and many of their followers in the movement of which Whichcote had been an early pioneer. Without shutting their eyes to the great amount of actual selfishness and inhumanity in the world, they devoted much effort, nevertheless, to picturing the heart of man as "naturally" good in the sense that when left to its own native impulses it tends invariably to humane and sensible feelings.
>
> There can be little question that this optimistic appraisal of human nature was in part a manifestation of the revolt against Puritanism . . . . It would hardly have been possible had it not been for their vigorous insistence, against the one-sided Augustinianism of the Lutheran and Calvinistic traditions, that man was not completely depraved as a result of the Fall, that he has still some natural power of doing good, that "nature" can co-operate with "grace" to the end of his salvation. But this is only part of the story; and what chiefly provoked them to their frequent declarations of man's "natural goodness" was undoubtedly not so much their enmity to the

Puritans as their zeal for combatting the dangerous political and moral doctrines of Thomas Hobbes.

Irving Babbitt in his *Rousseau and Romanticism* gives a similar account:

> The assertion of man's natural goodness is to be understood as a rebound from the total depravity that was held by the more austere type of Christian. This doctrine had even in the early centuries of the faith awakened certain protests like that of Pelagius, but for an understanding of the Rousseauistic protest one does not need to go beyond the great deistic movement of the early eighteenth century. God, instead of being opposed to nature, is conceived by the Deists as a power that expresses his goodness and loveliness through nature, including human nature. He not only sees virtue in instinct but inclines to turn virtue into a "sense," or instinct. And this means in practice to put emotional expansion in the place of spiritual concentration as the basis of life and morals.

The process by which the doctrine of the total depravity of man was replaced by the doctrine of the natural goodness of man, as Crane and Babbitt describe it, did much to abet the de-Christianizing process. Never before in the intellectual history of the Western world had there been so wide agreement among intellectuals as in the 18th and 19th centuries of the sinlessness of man in his natural state. And yet virtually all the fundamental doctrines of Christianity depend upon the doctrine of Original Sin, however interpreted, so that this new estimate of man's natural virtues struck directly at the heart of Christianity. How thoroughly English thought after 1775 succumbed to the doctrine of the natural goodness of man with its emphasis upon sentimentality, original genius, and the "beautiful soul," is evident from the difficulty in finding influential intellectuals who upheld the doctrine of sin, either original or unoriginal. Samuel Johnson was one and Edmund Burke was another, but their thinking had become almost anachronistic.

Rousseau, reacting violently to his calvinistic heritage, is probably more than any other writer responsible for turning intellectuals away from natural reason and toward natural feeling. It was no longer a question of whether the truth was to be found in Revelation or in reason but whether it was to be found in reason or in feeling. There can be no doubt of Rousseau's position:

Reasoning, he declared, "far from enlightening us, blinds us; it does not raise our soul, it enervates and corrupts the judgment, which it should perfect." "A thinking man is a depraved animal." Thus Rousseau's sentiments on the value of reason echo Luther's. But whereas Luther placed his trust in God and the Scriptures, Rousseau placed his trust in man and his feelings. For Rousseau, man is not so sinful that only God can save him; he is so good that he can save himself. "There is no sin in the human heart," he insisted: the doctrine of Original Sin is "a blasphemy." Rousseau admitted that sometimes he himself felt dizzy with virtue; he had an exquisite sense of his own sinlessness.

Rousseau had a long list of predecessors in the earlier 18th and even the latter part of the 17th century who were moving in his direction. "The man of feeling" had been celebrated for some time, but no one succeeded in selling the idea more forcefully or more attractively than Rousseau, through confessions and novels and his educational treatise, *Émile*. He made faith in man's emotions so irresistible that perhaps more than any other writer it was he who put the rationalists out of their misery.

When the oil of Hume's skepticism is added to Rousseau's fires, reason turns to ashes. For Hume, having come quite a different route, the route of rationalism itself, arrived at the same point as Rousseau. Hume used reason to destroy reason just as Rousseau used feeling to destroy reason, and neither was willing to allow the superior authority of religion. Men were now left not only without religion to guide them but also without reason: they had only their feelings.

3. Scientism

But all the while there were certain other developments in the intellectual history of Europe which in time were to deprive men even of their feelings and to leave them with only their senses to guide them. This phenomenon is due to the increasing trust that intellectuals were placing in the senses, in the scientific method, as the ultimate means of arriving at the truth.

As we have seen, the senses had been regarded almost universally as untrustworthy sources of truth during the Middle Ages, not only because they had been dulled by the Fall but because they had been denigrated by Plato's epistemology. But the scientific discoveries of Copernicus, Gilbert, Galileo, Kepler, Harvey, and Newton, among others in the 16th and 17th centuries, were so spectacular that the senses as a means to truth began to command a respect hitherto unknown in the intellectual history of Europe. Francis Bacon saw the prospects, even before most of these scientists had discovered anything, and his writings called attention to what seemed like a new way of arriving at truth. In his *Advancement of Learning* he explained how knowledge had been impeded because men would not trust their senses; in his *Novum Organum* he showed men how they should employ their senses systematically in order to discover the truth; and in his *New Atlantis*, he projected a scientific utopia which would remind men how close to a heaven on earth they could come if they were to harness the knowledge that their senses could bring to them.

The very fact that Bacon died of a fever brought on by an experiment in refrigeration in which he tried to freeze a chicken in the snow rather symbolized the new scientific spirit. But Bacon was by no means an atheist. All knowledge was, for him, "for the Glory of God and relief of man's estate." He never doubted that God was the author of all, and in true Christian fashion he gave Him due allegiance; but perhaps more than any other single intellectual, he spread the scientific spirit around Europe. In England, The Royal Society was dedicated to the discovery of truth through science, and Bacon's works were their scientific bible. The trouble was that as the century progressed, scientific intellectuals became more interested in "the relief of man's estate" than in the glory of God. At least they preferred to discover God through His world than through His words. It wasn't until later that they concluded that He wasn't in His world, nor indeed anywhere else.

And yet, even though the 18th century was a good deal more scientific-minded than the 17th, its discoveries were not so spectacular as those of the 17th. There was indeed plenty of scientific activity, as suggested by the achievements of Herschel and Laplace in astronomy, Galvani and Volta in physics, Priestley and Lavoisier in chemistry, Linnaeus in botany, and Buffon and Lamarck in bilogy, as well as Condillac in psychology and Jenner and Boerhaave in medicine. But somehow their contributions to science seemed less dramatic, less shattering to old beliefs than those of Galileo, Harvey, and Newton. It was as if science were holding back in order to let reason have its century before overtaking it in the next. Nor did 18th-century science seem quite the threat to religion that 19th-century science was to be. There was no Darwinism yet to undermine the religious view of man, and scientists in the 18th century on the whole did not attack religion so bluntly or devastatingly as they were to do in the 19th. But intellectuals in the 18th century became caught up in the scientific spirit more than ever before. Locke's thinking bore the stamp of the scientific spirit, and the atheistic materialism of the *philosophes* was to do quite as much for the scientific spirit as for the rationalist spirit. The way for the 19th-century onslaught against the authority of religion by scientifically oriented intellectuals was being well prepared.

Thus it seemed that all the intellectual trends which followed the Renaissance and in fact which originated during the Renaissance were challenging the authority of religion and Revelation. Any departure from a strict fideism seemed to open a Pandora's box. If a little learning was indeed a dangerous thing, then to drink deep in the well of learning seemed even more dangerous. If it were granted that man's unaided reason might lead to a few truths, why might it not lead to all truths? If men's feelings could be trusted in some matters, why not in all matters? And if the senses could solve the mysteries of nature, why could they not solve the mysteries of human nature? It seems not to be within a man's capacity to know where to draw the line between what only men can know and what only God can know. The more men come to trust their own wisdom the more they tend to doubt God's, even to the point that in time they doubt whether there is a God. The phenomenon of Renaissance humanism, it turns out, was merely a stop along the way between the point where men trusted only God's word to the point where they trusted only man's word. By the end of the 18th century, professional reasoners tended to put their ultimate trust in reason, professional feelers were putting their trust in feeling, professional scientists were putting their trust in the senses, and none were putting their trust in God.

But neither the Catholic nor the Protestant churches took these 17th- and 18th-century blows against orthodoxy without hitting back. In England the deists did not have everything their own way, nor was all the intellectual talent on their side. In fact, the reaction to the deists' proposal to reduce Christianity to rubble was sometimes astonishing. The fact that Tindal's chief work, for example, drew some 150 replies indicates something of the outrage of orthodoxy. Highly educated clergymen from all quarters put forth their best rhetoric and much sound sense in defending the Church.

The renowned Bishop George Berkeley, for example, warned that latitudinarianism would lead to deism, then to atheism, and then to moral collapse, and he pointed out that the doctrine of the Trinity is no more absurd than the mathematician's surd. Bishop William Warburton, an accomplished controversialist, dazzled his readers with a two-volume display of erudition in which he took on all the free-thinkers, past and present; and Joseph Butler in 1736 published *The Analogy of Religion, Natural and Revealed, to the Constitution and Course of Nature*, which was to remain for a century the most persuasive argument for Christianity in the face of all its opponents.

Some English defenders of the Faith bypassed the controversy between reason and Revelation and simply appealed to men's piety and religious feeling. William Law had played a substantial role in fighting off the deists' treatises with his own, but he at last settled for a quiet approach by writing *A Serious Call to a Devout and Holy Life* (1729), which Samuel Johnson called "the finest piece of hortatory theology in any language." John Wesley was interested not so much in answering the deists as in revitalizing Christianity, and he did so with such temporary success that it seemed that Christianity would prevail in England after all.

In France, where the enemies of Christianity were

less gentle, the Church was also less gentle. Catholicism had had far more practice in dealing with heretics and unbelievers than the Protestants, for whom burning and censoring and excommunicating were more appropriate for witches. But by the 17th century in France the Church had gone back to burning heretical books rather than their authors, and by the 18th century even excommunication had become rarer. Censorship was still extremely common, though it was often as much political as religious, since the two were not easily separated. And yet somehow even the most virulent attacks upon Christianity got through. The works of the *philosophes* were among the most popular and the most commonly forbidden, but wherever the danger seemed particularly great, there were ways of evading the censors, including publishing in foreign countries. Voltaire sometimes signed his diatribes against the Church with the names of dead persons, and on occasion even replied to his own attacks upon the Church in order to throw the authorities off the scent.

The crusade of the *philosophes* against religion drew a flood of responses from Catholic quarters. Between 1715 and 1789, some 900 works in defense of Christianity were published in France including 90 in a single year (1770). Refutations of the anti-religious writings of Diderot, Helvétius, and Rousseau were among the most threatening. Nor were these defenses of French Catholicism the works of incompetents. An ex-Jesuit, Abbé Nonnotte, famous for his erudition, contributed a prodigious work entitled *The Errors of Voltaire*, which went through four editions in its first year. And a parish priest by the name of Nicholas Sylvester Bergier took on the whole opposition. His *Deism Refutes Itself* (1765) was his answer to Rousseau, and his *Certainty of the Proofs of Christianity* (1767) was praised by the Pope. In his *Apology of the Chris-*

tian Religion he took on the Baron d'Holbach and won a pension large enough so that he could devote full time to defending the Church. He then proceeded to blast d'Holbach again in a huge work entitled *An Examination of Materialism.*

The Jesuit Guillaume Francois Berthier, one of the most accomplished defenders of religion against the French Enlighteners, provided a running commentary on the theological and philosophical errors of the *Encyclopédie* as it appeared volume by volume, often in a more scholarly fashion than the encyclopedists themselves. He also attacked Voltaire's anti-religious works and succeeded in engaging the great man in open controversy. Voltaire, however, may have won more by his wit than his wisdom as is suggested by his premature account of Berthier's death in *An Account of the Illness, Confession, Death, and Apparition of the Jesuit Berthier,* in which he described how Berthier died of a fit of yawning over the edition of his own periodical *The Journal of Trevoux.*

But neither all the wit nor all the wisdom were on the side of the *philosophes*. Elie Catherine Fréron was perhaps the greatest scholar and rhetorician of all the defenders of the Faith in Catholic France. In some 30 volumes in approximately the same number of years he launched a one-man crusade against all the *philosophes*. He was drawn into personal attacks and intemperate arguments, not so much by his own inclinations as by those of his opponents. The case against the unbelieving intellectuals was not limited to treatises and solemn articles in journals. One of the most successful comedies of the 1760 season in Paris was a play entitled *Les Philosophes* by Charles Palissot de Monteney, which with relish and skill caricatured Helvétius and Diderot and Rousseau.

It is difficult to communicate the nature and extent of the war between the believers and unbelievers in Enlightenment Europe. It was often sincere and scholarly, often vengeful and savage, often witty, and sometimes amusing if not ridiculous; but in the intellectual history of the Western world there was hardly any controversy that was more important. The stakes were the survival of religion in the minds of intellectuals who were to determine the intellectual climate for the decades and centuries to come. If religion was as crucial as its defenders said it was, then the survival of civilization could be in question. If it was as serious a hindrance to civilization as its opponents said it was, then a new and brighter age could be in the offing.

Reduced to its essence the issues were something like the following: The defenders of Christianity insisted not only that there is a God but that He spoke to men through the Scriptures. Men have immortal souls and God sent His Son to teach them how to save them. The unbelievers by contrast insisted that there is no God, at least no personal God, that the authors of the Bible received no more divine aid than any other authors, so that there is no basis for believing that Christ is our Savior and hence that the Church teaches the truth. There is no Heaven, no Hell, no Salvation, and when a man dies the burdocks grow over his grave and that is an end of him. Furthermore, men don't need religion or the church because their own faculties, especially their reason and their senses can ultimately bring them the peace and happiness that they all yearn for. Religion, so far from being the comfort and hope of mankind, is a major cause of misery and suffering. It holds back progress and breeds destructive superstitions which only enlightened reason can clear away.

The controversy was exacerbated by the fact that the role of secular intellectuals in the intellectual history of the Western world was increasing. As we have seen, the intellectual life of the Middle Ages, both early and late, still lay almost wholly in the hands of churchmen, despite the fact that Tertullian, himself a layman, and Pelagius argued for an increased role for laymen in the life of the Church. During the Renaissance learned laymen played a much larger role, so large in fact that most of what is read from the Renaissance period today was written by laymen, particularly as a result of the restoration to respectability of poetry and the drama. Many Renaissance scholars and educators and philosophers and scientists were also laymen. But even so, in the broad outlines of the intellectual history of the Renaissance, the most influential intellectuals still came in good part from the ranks of the clergy. The overwhelming majority of Renaissance intellectuals were Christians, and since religious learning was still regarded as the highest kind of learning, the churchmen who possessed it to a higher degree than non-churchmen were still the chief guardians of the truth.

But whereas most influential lay intellectuals during the Renaissance were friends of Christianity, large numbers of them in the later 17th and the 18th century were not. It is perhaps not possible to show that there is a close relationship between the rise of secular intellectuals and the decline of the influence of religion in the thinking of intellectuals, but there can be no doubt that the Church was beginning to relinquish its intellectual leadership to secular intellectuals in the 18th century. The names of George Berkeley, Joseph Butler, William Law, Berthier and Fréron do not figure so strongly in the intellectual history of Europe as do those of Hume, Kant, Voltaire, and Rousseau.

As the controversy between believing and unbelieving intellectuals continued in the 19th century, the unbelieving intellectuals became more and more intellectual and more unbelieving; and the defenders of Christianity became more unbelieving but less intellectual so that if religion was losing out slowly in the uneducated circles of Europe, it was losing out rapidly in intellectual circles, where it may have mattered most. Furthermore, as the most influential intellectuals became increasingly certain that the answer to the eternal questions could be found, if not in reason, then in science, they stepped up their attack upon the authority of religion and of the Church, so that there was a steady movement from deism to atheism to anti-theism as the intellectual leadership of the Western world passed from churchmen to non-churchmen to anti-churchmen.

CHAPTER V

THE RISE OF THE ANTI-THEISTS

As intellectual history in Western Europe passed from the 18th to the 19th century, deism had already developed to a remarkable degree into atheism and was now to pass from atheism to anti-theism. If it is possible to distinguish between atheism and anti-theism, atheism may be said to describe the position that there is no God without necessarily insisting that religion is the chief obstacle to man's happiness. Anti-theism, on the other hand, regards religion as the bane of civilization, the chief source of man's misery, the main impediment to progress and social reform. Anti-theism thus proposes the abolition of religion as the first step in the advancement of civilization. This distinction seems useful because it suggests how far the process of the de-Christianizing of the intellectuals was to go, and hence how far they would have to return if ever they were to be re-Christianized.

The *philosophes* of the later 18th-century France may be said to be anti-theists by any definition of the term, and they were as uncompromising perhaps as any 19th-century anti-theist; but the *philosophes* were still *avant garde* in their frontal attacks upon religion and the Church, and they were still plentifully opposed by churchmen and other Christian intellectuals with extraordinary talents. Furthermore, the influence of genuine 18th-century anti-theists like Diderot, d'Holbach, and LaMettrie, was not so devastating to religion as that of the giant anti-theists of the 19th-century.

The case against Christianity which French intellectuals had been building up in the 18th century was in the long run to be solidified in the 19th. But it is important to recognize that even in early 19th-century France the spirit of the Enlightenment did not go unopposed. There was a group of French intellectuals, for example, in the early decades of the 19th-century who were convinced that the Enlightenment led to the French Revolution and that the French Revolution was an unmitigated disaster.

Included among these was one of the great minds of early 19th-century France, namely, Francois-René de Chateaubriand, who came out in favor of Christianity in the face of the anti-theism of all the *philosophes*. Chateaubriand's remarkable early education was for the priesthood, but the skepticism of the age overtook him and he soon professed himself a free-thinker, if not an atheist. It was not, however, his free-thinking that led him back to Christianity but the deaths of his mother and sister. "These two voices from the tomb . . . were a blow to me," he declared. "I became a Christian . . . and I believed." The ripest fruits of this renewed belief was his celebrated book *The Genius of Christianity* (1802), in which he turned his already-tested rhetorical powers to the service of religion. It was a stirring defense of Christianity in which Chateaubriand demonstrated to any reasonable reader how crucial Christianity was to Western civilization, how superior it was to the pagan religions, how irresistible its aesthetic appeal; and he prefaced this eloquent defense by assuring the reader that he now believed in all the fundamental doctrines of Christianity. He called himself an *anti-philosophe*, and he proceeded on the assumption that France was full of *anti-philosophes*, who, like him, had had enough of the brittle rationalism of the Enlightenment and the excesses of the French Revolution in general and of Napoleon in particular. Judging from the enthusiastic reception of the book he must have been right. Even Napoleon himself, whose sworn enemy Chateaubriand was to become, had a good word for it: It is "a work of lead and gold," he declared, "but the gold predominates." If exhuberance and exaggeration flawed Chateaubriand's defense of religion, it may have been those qualities which most endeared it to its readers. A half century later his countryman, Jules Lemaitre, called it over-generously, "The greatest success in the history of French literature."

As a French defender of Christianity in post-revolutionary times, Chateaubriand had the support of the Traditionalists, an ultra-conservative group of French intellectuals who were largely ultramontanists, i.e., they insisted upon the supremacy of the papacy over all national churches and governments. Among them was Count Joseph de Maistre, who observed that "the philosophy of the last century will form in the eyes of posterity one of the most shameful epochs of the human spirit" and that it was "in fact nothing but a veritable system of practical atheism." He deplored the rationalism of 18th-century French intellectuals and he reminded them that the tradition of Catholicism is simply the fulfillment of the covenant God gave to Abraham, passed on to Moses, and then to Aaron and so on down to the promise made to Peter. In his work *On the Papacy* (1817) he reaffirmed that the Catholic Church is a divine institution, that Peter was the first pope, and that Christ Himself conferred inherited powers on Peter's successors. De Maistre even insisted on the idea of papal infallibility before it was made a doctrine by the First Vatican Council.

Other French intellectuals also turned their talents

and learning to defending the Christian faith, including Viscomte de Bonald and Felicité Robert de Lamennais, who were *anti-philosophes* in the extreme. Lamennais became so uncompromising an ultramontanist that even Rome condemned him, and Bonald was so strongly in favor of absolutism in matters of Church and State (and the rule of the State by the Church) that he refused to recognize the achievement of Greek art because it was created in a democracy.

But such protestations against the Enlighteners' attacks on Christianity and such passionate reaffirmations of the authority of the Catholic Church and the Papacy did not prevent the anti-theists from prevailing in 19th-century France. As intellectuals became increasingly sure of their own powers and increasingly doubtful of God's, attacks on religion became louder and more insistent.

It was to be thinkers like Auguste Comte, Emile Littré, Ernest Renan, and Hippolyte Adolphe Taine who pointed toward France's intellectual future, not Chateaubriand or the Traditionalists.

It was Auguste Comte who, more than anyone else, got French intellectuals back on the anti-theistic track. Despite, or perhaps because of, his Catholic upbringing, Comte announced at age 14 that he had "naturally ceased to believe in God," and he then proceeded to demonstrate in his celebrated essay on *The Law of the Three Stages*, how outmoded Christianity and indeed all religion had become. In the first or primitive stage of civilization, he explained, men relied primarily on religion and Revelation for the truth about the human condition; then, as civilization developed, it entered the second or transitional stage in which the method of philosophy replaced Revelation; and finally, in its most advanced stage, civilization repudiates not only religion but reason, and seeks the truth wholly from the scientific method, i.e., the method of the senses. The historical account of man's epistemological development provides the rationale for Comte's positivism, which holds roughly that if you can't see it, hear it, touch it, taste it, or smell it, you can't believe it.

In Comte's view, there is no place for God in this third, final, and most enlightened stage. Even in the second stage, belief in God, like belief in elves and fairies, was overthrown by the power of reason, he observed. And indeed historically, as we have seen, that is what happened when the Age of Faith, which lasted some 5,000 years, was replaced by the Age of Reason, which lasted perhaps a century and a half. But the Age of Science, the advent of which Comte was announcing, was to give the *coup de grâce* to God. Since God cannot be detected by the senses He therefore cannot be said to exist. Any continued insistence on belief in God or the doctrines of Christianity is to be regarded as a holdover or a reversion to the first or primitive stage of civilization. Atheism, Comte insisted, is the sign of a mature civilization. He believed in a scientific elite, and he looked forward to the day when engineers would replace priests and mathematicians would replace philosophers. Not only the science of nature but the science of man, the sociology of man without God, was to mark the third and final stage of civilization. Such, then, was the Comtean spirit—the triumph of science over religion and metaphysics—and such was the reassertion of French anti-theism.

So original and powerful a thinker as Comte was bound to spawn disciples both in and out of France. Among his most sympathetic countrymen was Émile Littré, a student of medicine, a lexicographer, and, in his early years, an orthodox Christian. By the time Littré had read Comte's *Course of Positive Philosophy*, however, he was already on the road to atheism and Comte helped him along. "His book conquered me," he declared. "I became from then on a disciple of the positive philosophy, and such I have remained." Littré, together with the famous French physiologist Claude Bernard, exemplify the way in which positivism was pushing God out of man's consciousness. It was not so much a question as to whether God existed or not, but a matter of asserting that only verified empirical data can be trusted as the way to truth; and since God will not submit to the verifiable-empirical-data test, questions of His existence are not even to be asked. Like Comte before them, they were convinced that manifestations of God through the Sacred Scriptures and tradition and logic must be discounted. Bernard was himself so distrustful even of philosophy that he objected to Comte's attempt to develop a dogmatic system out of his positivistic view of knowledge. The truly empirical approach to reality, he insisted, cannot be encompassed in a system. In fact, in the longrun Comte's legacy was not his "system" with its emphasis upon the evolution of the sciences of mathematics, physics, chemistry, biology, and sociology; it was his spirit and his method.

Two of the most influential French intellectuals to follow in Comte's wake were Taine and Renan, and both in their separate ways advanced the prestige of the scientific method at the expense of the authority of Christianity. Taine, the great philosopher, psychologist, historian, and literary critic shed his belief in Christianity at age 15, and in order not to live perpetually in a state of skepticism and doubt, he embraced the scientism that he found all around him. He kept, however, a warm place in his heart for metaphysics, which Comte said a man should outgrow, and he spent the rest of his life trying to reconcile philosophy with science. But of one thing he was certain: he believed with Comte that a man should certainly repudiate religion. This refusal to recognize the authority of religion permeates all his very considerable learning and writings, though he was not devoted, as other French atheists and positivists were at the time, to systematically destroying the doctrines of Christianity.

Renan, on the other hand, also a man of immense learning, would not leave religion alone. He was its enemy the whole of his intellectual life. In his *Life of Jesus* (1863) and his *History of the Origins of Christianity* (1863-83) he divested Christ of all supernatural claims made for His life and hence contributed, in his own spectacular way, to killing off Christianity. As early as 1846, when Renan was 23 years old, he proudly announced his conclusion that "there is no perceptible action of a free will superior to that of man," and in his *Dialogues* 30 years later he observed with true positivistic logic that "A being who does not reveal himself by any act is for science a being that does not exist."

Such then are some of the sentiments against religion of some of the most influential 19-century French thinkers. The influence, as we shall see, was to continue on into the 20th century.

Intellectuals in England, meanwhile, were making their own often highly original efforts to put an end to religion. William Paley at the end of the 18th century had made a valiant effort to counteract the skepticism of Hume by writing a 2-volume work entitled *A View of the Evidences of Christianity*, in which he rested his case for the truth of Christianity on the witnesses and miracles of early Christianity, and then he started off the 19th century with another work, this time on *Natural Theology*, (1802), in which he attempted to prove the existence of God by appealing merely to natural phenomena, as if he recognized that his *Evidences of Christianity* might not suffice in an increasingly skeptical and scientific age.

But it was too late. The rampage of deism, seemingly the arguments of Hume, the influence of the *philosophes*, and the surge of scientism, all pointed in the direction of a continued attack among English intellectuals on the authority of revealed religion. Even in the early 19th century attacks on religion were the order of the day. Shelley published his adolescent pamphlet on *The Necessity of Atheism*, but his father-in-law, Charles Godwin, not so innocently attacked all Christian institutions as the curse of civilization. Of greater consequence was the position of the Utilitarians on the subject of religion. Prudence more than anything else prevented them from being included among the most spectacular anti-theists of their century. They were already regarded as sufficiently radical in their economic and social views without taking on the Church of England as well. But there can be no doubt about where they stood on religion. Jeremy Bentham and George Grote wrote a little book, supposedly by "Philip Beauchamp," in which religion was subjected to the Utilitarian test, and needless to say, it came off badly. On the pleasure-pain scale, they concluded that religion clearly produced more pain than pleasure, and hence was, by definition, not useful, and therefore false. Furthermore, since no one had ever testified to the existence of immortality, or to the joys of heaven, Christianity denied too much pleasure in this life for too little evidence of pleasure in the next. The perpetual threat of Hell, which was vividly presented in Christianity, and the promise of Heaven, which was so vague and even doubtful, made religion seem not only useless but vicious. The possibility that God had spoken to man through the Scriptures, whether usefully or not, was not even to be entertained. Besides, reason could lead men to virtue more surely and less painfully than religion.

Thus Jeremy Bentham gave up the doctrines of Christianity and the Christian ethics that derive from them in return for the ancient hedonistic concept of the pleasure-pain principle of the second and third-rate pagan philosophers which Aristotle and Plato had roundly refuted, and which were totally incompatible with all the great religions. James Mill, Bentham's atheistic disciple, attempted to improve on Bentham's ethical system using the same premises but without notable success, and even his son, John Stuart Mill, who perceived at least some of the problems connected with Utilitarianism, was not thereby turned to Christianity. "I am one of the very few examples in the country," he declared in his *Autobiography*, "of one who had not thrown off religion, but never had it." Mill was appalled by the limitations of Utilitarianism, but he was even more appalled by the doctrines of Christianity.

No event in the 19th century did more to support Comte's declaration that the third and final stage of civilization, the scientific stage, had arrived than the publication of Darwin's *On the Origin of Species*. The timing and the manner of presentation were devastatingly effective. The impact of Darwinism on religion did not, however, come from Darwin's own unbelief. He had in fact prepared to take orders in the Anglican Church but his scientific interests led to continuous postponement until at length he lost his faith in the Old Testament, then the miracles of the New Testament, and finally in Christianity generally; and gradually he took an agnostic stance, without, however, participating in the crusade against religion which some of his fellow intellectuals were conducting.

After the initial shock of Darwin's doctrine of natural selection and evolution began to wear off, scientists and social scientists perceived that the pessimistic implications were unwarranted. In fact they saw so many optimistic prospects in biological development that they began to apply Darwin's doctrines to every area of human endeavor. Intellectuals everywhere caught fire at the notion that everything is evolving, everything is progressing. "As natural selection works solely by and for the good of each being," Darwin observed, "all corporal and mental endowments will tend to progress towards perfection." Darwin had come to this conclusion not through religious belief or through reason, but through scientific observation. The scientific method was indeed then the way to the truth and not only to the truth but to the long-sought earthly utopia. In the minds of many intellectuals who were won over to Darwinian optimism, religion had always been the chief barrier to progress and perfection. Societies can best evolve, they believed, if unencumbered by religion. And so there was no lack of intellectuals to interpret Darwin and to turn his biological theories into social theories, intellectuals as learned as they were persuasive, like Thomas Huxley and Herbert Spencer and Walter Bagehot. Clearly the scientific spirit was well on its way to overtaking not only the religious spirit in England but the rational spirit.

Compared to the French and English, German intellectuals were slow in shedding Christianity. Even the German Enlightenment was, relatively speaking, Christian. Pietism and mysticism and even scholasticism were important elements in late 17th- and early 18th-century German thought. While England, Holland, and France were producing Hobbes, Newton, Spinoza, and Descartes, who mark unmistakable departures from Christian orthodoxy as popularly perceived, Germany was producing Leibnitz, whose thought remained Christian-oriented, who did not like the anti-Christian implications of Spinoza's ideas, and who, in his late years, even sought to dispel a Jesuit's doubts about the doctrine of transubstantiation.

Christian Thomasius, the first important intellectual of the German Enlightenment, underwent a spiritual conversion which led him to German pietism. It was after his conversion in 1694 that he wrote his most important work, and he was concluding that ultimate truth can be found only in the Bible at a time when most of the other important intellectuals of Europe were concluding that it could be found almost anywhere except the Bible. Needless to say, however, Thomasius did not represent the wave of the future in German thought. Nor did the philosophers of feeling, like Franz von Baader, who remained true to Catholicism, and Fredrick Schleiermacher, who remained true to Protestantism. No more did Heine, who failed so miserably in his attempt to become an atheist that before his life was over he fell fully back into faith. And Goethe himself never left his faith, though he didn't much help the Christian cause by insisting from time to time that it didn't so much matter what religion a man believed, so long as he was religious.

But the point to be made here about German intellectuals is that, though they were de-Christianized later than those of the rest of Western Europe, they numbered among them the most effective anti-theists of the 19th century. The de-Christianizing of German intellectuals began quietly enough with the gentle deism of Kant, who, in his book *Religion Within the Bounds of Mere Reason* (1793), did as much to downgrade the fundamental Christian doctrines as Locke had done more than a century earlier in his *Reasonableness of Christianity*. Kant satisfied himself in the *Critique of Pure Reason* that the old theoretical proofs of God were no longer tenable, and yet, being convinced that men need moral guidance, he established a metaphysics of voluntarism and so reduced religiousness to morality. His Categorical Imperative, which insisted that men must be good because they *must*, and which held that an act has moral value only when its motive is worthy of becoming a law for all reasonable beings, was intended to supplant the commandments of Moses and Christ, and as such placed great faith, no doubt too great faith, in human nature. So Kant turned out to be a sentimental romantic in disguise, and in the process of his cogitations gutted the authority of Christianity.

Still another step in the de-Christianizing of German intellectuals was the thinking of Hegel. Hegel started out in the Lutheran fold, and in his *Early Theological Works* he acknowledged the crucial role of religion in life: "Religion is one of the important concerns in our lives," he wrote. "Already as children we are taught to stammer prayers to the Godhead," and "when we mature, preoccupation with religion fills a good part of our lives." But Hegel's preoccupation with Lutheranism led him to recognize that religion interfered seriously with his freedom of thought. The fear of God which the Bible said was the beginning of wisdom meant for Hegel the end of thought; and so in order not to give up thought he gave up Christianity and all faith in a personal God; for a personal God meant, in his view, a tyrant-God. He developed a bitterness against the authority of the Church, and he regarded Christianity, with its faith in a personal God, as the true enemy of truth. The God of the Old Testament, he declared, is "a demon of hate," and Christianity, though professing to be a religion of love, reverted to the spirit of the Old Testament.

In these conclusions Hegel found support in Kant, but he found even Kant's moral imperative too confining. And yet Hegel had no desire to be an atheist, and he refused to become a pantheist. In his late years he even argued, in his own peculiar way, on the proofs of the existence of God.

German mainline philosophical thought was clearly moving toward atheism and was to move quickly toward anti-theism, as it developed from the pietism of Thomasius, the Protestantism of Schleiermacher, and the Catholicism of von Baader to the deism of Kant and the doubtful deism of Hegel. It achieved such glories as belong to the atheistic state in the thought of Arthur Schopenhauer, whom Nietzsche called the first true atheist. Schopenhauer was contemptuous of the pussyfooting pantheism and the deistic deviousness of the philosophy that preceeded him. These efforts to dismiss religion without the courage to come out for atheism Schopenhauer regarded as intellectual cowardice, and he was no coward. He found the idea of being face-to-face with a universal and personal God to be intolerable, because there was no way, as he saw it, to reconcile human freedom with divine freedom, and he insisted on human freedom, indeed on the supremacy of the human will, and the notion that there should be anything between theism and atheism was incomprehensible. Theism was an albatross around the neck of the free-spirited intellectual, and he would have none of it. He therefore opted for atheism, and was later to be much applauded by thinkers such as Burkhardt and Nietzsche for intellectual boldness and courage.

The marvellous ambiguity of Hegel's philosophy inspired a few Christian thinkers, but it inspired many more atheistic thinkers. The Hegelians of the Right, who saw in him an uncanny fusion of reason and religion were, in the long run, less important. The Left Hegelians, on the other hand, marked the direction in which German philosophy was to go, and included not only Bruno Bauer, David Strauss, and Ludwig Feuerbach, but also Marx and Engels, all of whom, together with Nietzsche, and such materialists as Vogt and Buchner, suggest that Germany had produced the most dazzling galaxy of anti-theists of any nation in 19th-century Europe.

Strauss's and Bauer's contribution to the de-Christianizing of the intellectuals was particularly significant because they were theologians and religious historians, and hence their attacks on Christianity could carry weight in a way that secular scholars' thought could not. In his spectacular work in *The Life of Jesus Critically Examined* (1853-56) Strauss proceeded to demonstrate that Christ was no more than a man like any other man and that any supra-rational or supernatural significance attached to him was merely an expression of the human need to create and perpetuate myths. There was still enough religion left in Germany, however, so that for his pains Strauss was dismissed from the University of Tubingen where he had been lecturing and forced into permanent retirement from university life. Large numbers of intellectuals in Europe had already come to the same conclusion about Christ and the Bible, but for the most part they were not scriptural scholars nor religious historians; and by the middle of the 19th century many intellectuals, especially the Left Hegelians, were delighted to have the support of Strauss in their own intellectual undertakings.

These included particularly Feuerbach, who was also a theologian as well as a philosopher, and who sharpened his rhetorical teeth at the age of 26 on a work entitled *Thoughts on Death and Immortality*, in which he attacked Christianity as egotistic and inhumane. He then proceeded to sort out the contradictions in Hegel and concluded that Hegel was, or rather should have been, a materialist; and then, with his interpretation of Hegel in hand, he wrote his most celebrated work, *The Essence of Christianity*, in which he came to much the same conclusion as Strauss, but with a much broader philosophical base. He attracted the attention of Marx and Engels, as well as a whole host of Russian intellectuals who had been waiting for someone like Feuerbach to come along to stimulate their own suspicions that reason and science rather than religion are the way to the truth and the only way to *any* truth concerning the human condition.

Marx was so influential an intellectual that his view of religion is extremely important to our study. His view was that all religions should be condemned. He was convinced that religion was a bourgeois invention to keep the proletariat in chains; furthermore, religion taught that the only paradise was in the next world, whereas Marx hoped to establish a paradise in this. Religion, Marx insisted, teaches men to be content with their lot, whereas they ought to devote their energies to improving their lot. Hence his famous phrase that religion is "the opiate of the people". It is therefore superfluous to inquire whether Marx believed that God spoke to man through the Bible, or whether he approved the authority of the Church. "The religion of the workers has no God," Marx declared, "because it seeks to restore the dignity of man."

In the mode of the prevailing intellectual atmosphere of 19th-century Europe, Marx drew from the leading atheistic thinkers in England, France, and in his native Germany to conclude that the ultimate truth lay in philosophy and science and that it was within man's natural goodness to rearrange society so that, without religion, a real-life utopia is possible. Most influential disciples of Marx have been religiously faithful in observing his teachings on religious faith.

If the de-Christianizing of the intellectuals in Germany was slow compared to England and France, it was even slower in Russia. Russia did not participate in the 18th-century Enlightenment any more than it participated in the Renaissance. Furthermore, Russian Orthodoxy held the minds of Russian intellectuals for more than a century after Catholic and Protestant Christianity had ceased to hold the minds of leading Western European intellectuals. Even in the earlier 19th century the way to truth, particularly among the slavophiles, like Kirēyevsky, Khomiakov, and Aksakov, was still through the Bible and the Church.

But once the de-Christianizing process took hold in Russia, it proceeded more rapidly even than in Germany. Russian intellectuals in ever greater numbers began studying in Western universities where they breathed in the heady air of rationalism, scientism, and materialism; then they returned to their native land full of zeal for the various gospels according to Hegel, Feuerbach, Marx, Vogt, Buchner, *et al.* The transformation of Christian intellectuals in Russia to anti-Christian intellectuals was so rapid and so complete that by the 1870's Dostoevsky was almost alone in his insistence that they were looking for the real truth about the human condition and human destiny in the wrong places. Even Tolstoy, who wanted no part of the scientism and materialism that had captured the minds and imaginations of the Russian intellectuals in the 1870's and '80's, insisted upon subjecting the Scriptures to his own reason, and despite his undoubted spirituality, he produced, in effect, the Gospel according to Tolstoy in his study entitled *Union and Translation of the Four Gospels.*

Needless to say, Dostoevsky and Tolstoy did not represent the main line of Russian thought during the last half of the 19th century. The main line passed through the chief atheists of Russia. And the conversion of some Russian intellectuals to atheism or virtual atheism was little short of dramatic. Chernyshevsky, Dobrolyubov, and Pisarev, for example, were deeply religious in their younger years, but Pisarev lost his faith almost overnight under the influence of such German materialists as Vogt and Buchner. Chernyshevsky, one of the major forerunners of Russian Communism, was a devout believer in 1848, but after reading Feuerbach's *Essence of Christianity* he became a devout unbeliever in 1849. Actually Feuerbach's anti-theism accounted for a good deal of the anti-Christian thinking of the 19th-century Russian intellectuals, including the great Belinsky, who couldn't read German but whose friends obligingly translated Feuerbach for him so that he could confirm his unbelief. Belinsky's *Letter to Gogol*, written as an impassioned response to Gogol's impassioned defense of Russian orthodoxy in his *Selected Correspondence with Friends*, though not wholly anti-Christian in tone, became the manifesto of Russian radical thought.

Alexander Hertsen, the chief 19th-century Russian intellectual in exile, also owed much of his unbelief to Feuerbach, and the anarchist Bakunin rejoiced to discover that Comte and Feuerbach had attained the state of atheism independently. He singled out Christianity as the worst of all possible religions because more fully than any other it guaranteed "the impoverishment, the enslavement, and the annihilation of mankind for the benefit of the deity."

The relatively sudden revolt against religion by 19th-century Russian intellectuals may in part be explained as a reaction to the extreme conservatism of Russian Orthodoxy and Russian Czardom. But German intellectuals, even more than their French and English counterparts, provided them with their sharpest weapons against both. In any case, the way for the intellectual acceptance of Marxism-Leninism in Russia was thoroughly prepared.

As the 19th century progressed, the ranks of Christian intellectuals in Europe thinned in the face of such massive opposition. Even Chateaubriand early in the century was aware how far religion had lost out in intellectual circles: "Who would now read a theological work?" he asks: "Only pious men who have no need to be convinced and true Christians who are already persuaded." And yet during the latter half of the 19th century some of the most effective voices in defense of Christianity where still to be heard from, voices so effective that they still echo in the late 20th century. They would include Newman, Kierkegaard, and Dostoevsky: a Catholic Christian, a Protestant Christian, and an Orthodox Christian. What they had most in common was a realization that they were living in a post-Christian age and they became passionate defenders of Christianity not merely because they were passionate Christians; they also feared that the man of reason and the man of science were destroying Christianity and that without Christianity Western civilization would lose its meaning, its order, and eventually its very life.

Newman in his best-known work, his *Apologia Pro Vita Sua*, was defending himself; but his works, taken together, constitute a brilliant defense of Christianity against the encroachments not only of liberal theology, which he perceived to be leading toward atheism, but against the atheistic bent of English utilitarianism and the spirit, not of science, but of scientism. As early as 1826 in the Oxford University Sermons on "The Theory of Religious Belief" he began in a quiet way to counter the prevailing drift into unbelief. His *Grammar of Assent* pursued the task farther. His efforts to counteract the influence of atheistic intellectuals was not by direct assault or by alarming the faithful but by attempting to strengthen the Church as the preserver of dogmatic religion, to shore up the intellectual bulwark of its traditions, and to renew the spiritual life of its institutions. In the process he concluded that there was nothing in the Church of England that was essentially incompatible with the Catholic Church: hence his *Tracts for the Times* and eventual conversion to Roman Catholicism. But even after his conversion, he never ceased his efforts to pit the forces of belief against the forces of unbelief, and in such works as the *Tamworth Reading Room Lectures* he more boldly took on the enemy in direct combat, particularly Jeremy Bentham, whose utilitarianism Newman felt to be a serious threat to religion, and Sir Robert Peel, who seemed to stand for the substitution of science and education for religious faith, and who thus represented a good many contemporary intellectuals.

Newman was as much concerned to save secular knowledge as he was to save religion, and in his *Idea of a University* he demonstrated how the former must depend on the latter. He was, in effect, reiterating the position of the Christian humanists in his belief in the compatibility of religion and the sciences. What he was doing that most of his fellow intellectuals were not doing was insisting that the secular disciplines were all handmaidens of religion and took their ultimate meaning from religion. His powerful rhetorical gifts are in part responsible for such influence as he has enjoyed both in his own and in the present century, and his arguments still will not quite go away.

Kierkegaard, like Newman, was a Christian gadfly in a post-Christian age. It is as if he had set out deliberately to bring discomfort to the intellectually comfortable. He especially went after those who had concluded that natural man is not sinful after all, that progress was therefore not only possible but probable, and that science could produce not only progress but happiness in a degree heretofore unknown to mankind. Kierkegaard's mind was operating on a quite different wavelength than that of the 19th-century European intellectuals who shared these delusions. Kierkegaard was preoccupied with suffering; not physical suffering, which science might help, but spiritual suffering, which science could not help, but which religion could.

Kierkegaard succeeded in demonstrating that life is rather more complex than the rationality of Hegel's ethical universe would have it. He insisted that man is a reservoir of emotions, including guilt, willfulness, anxiety, and above all, despair, whose role in human behavior Hegel and certainly Kant had not sufficiently taken into account. Kierkegaard's universe was furthermore diametrically opposed to the scientific universe of the intellectuals who were breathing in the spirit of Comte.

Just as Comte had his three stages, so Kierkegaard had his three stages, both in the development of civilization and of individual men. While Comte was explaining to the world that it had just passed through two stages of development, the religious and the metaphysical, and had at last arrived at the ultimate stage, the scientific, Kierkegaard explained that man might better go in the opposite direction, from aesthetic (hedonistic) man through ethical (rational) man to the highest stage, religious man. The lowest stage for Comte was the highest for Kierkegaard. The second stage, the philosophical stage, was a transitional stage for both, a stage to be passed through. The lowest stage for Kierkegaard, the aesthetic stage, was incomprehensible to Comte and the highest stage for Comte, science, was incomprehensible to Kierkegaard. While Comte was writing about the wonders of astronomy, mathematics, physics, chemistry, biology, and above all, sociology, Kierkegaard was writing *Fear and Trembling, Sickness unto Death*, and *The Concept of Dread*. Their thinking simply did not connect.

"Faith alone," Kierkegaard insisted, "can make man whole." Aesthetic man leads to boredom and despair; ethical man leads to doubt and insecurity. All men suffer from despair, whether they know it or not. It is the sickness unto death from which they can be rescued only by religion. Kierkegaard's argument was based not merely upon man's need for God but upon the conviction that God exists, that Christ is God Incarnate, and that the Bible is the voice of God. Belief, he declared, is not a matter for speculation or "a starting point for thought." Over and over again he insisted that religion is "a matter of a real individual face to face with a real God." And without faith in Christ, Kierkegaard insisted, all is vain. The "leap of faith," in Kierkegaard's view, was crucial if man was to avoid despair.

But it was not merely Kierkegaard's commitment to Christ and his inquiry into the problem of how to be a Christian that set him off from his intellectual brethren; it was also his existentialism, his subjectivity which insisted upon the fact of individual existence before all else. The emotional fervor, the high drama of Kierkegaard's most compelling writing is due in part to his personal spiritual struggles. He had chosen to become a Christian, and he was forever demonstrating to himself why he should remain a Christian and trying to understand what it meant to be a Christian. He got from his elderly father not only an excellent knowledge of Latin and Greek but a sense of the drama of Christian faith, partly because his father acted out for him stories and scenes which stimulated Kierkegaard's religious imagination. Kierkegaard also inherited from his father a deep-seated melancholy which runs through his writing, and which heightened his sense of guilt and sin and hence, sometimes, his despair. A particularly poignant event in Kierkegaard's life was his decision to break off his engagement to the 17-year-old Regine Olsen, which he did as a kind of spiritual renunciation and which he may have spent much of the rest of his life justifying. But whatever personal experiences account for the nature of Kierkegaard's religious thought, the fact seems to be that he wrote about facets of man's nature that most intellectuals of his century seemed unaware of and in a way that they were not capable of. Certainly there were not many of them to whom Abraham's willingness to sacrifice Isaac made sense as it made sense to Kierkegaard, for they spent their energies leaping away from faith, not toward it.

Perhaps no Christian intellectual in the 19th century including Kierkegaard was more acutely aware that he was taking on virtually the entire intellectual establishment in both western and eastern Europe than Dostoevsky. Almost all of Kierkegaard's works were in one way or another in the tradition of Christian apologetics if not polemics. But even Kierkegaard did not suffer from the messianic complex that was Dostoevsky's, and that complex was all the more messianic because he himself, unlike Kierkegaard, at one time partook of the radical, socialist utopian thinking which he came later to attack. He was born into a highly religious family, but like many another intellectual of his time in Russia he fell under the spell of radical Russian thinkers who had been trained in Europe. It was not enough that he should join the Petrashevsky Circle, which consisted mostly of theoretical radicals, but he also joined the Durov Group, within the Circle, which proposed radical political action, based on radical non-religious, if not atheistic, premises. He was in fact sent to prison partly for reading in public Belinsky's *Letter to Gogol*, which, as we have seen, was a kind of manifesto of radical and atheistic groups. But four years in prison and four more in the army taught him much about human nature and led him to conclude that men are not good enough to get along without God.

In his *Notes from the Underground*, he took on the entire Western intellectual establishment, which now included most Russian intellectuals who had joined it, if not surpassed it in their radical socialist utopian scientific rationalism. Ostensibly the work was an attack on Chernyshevsky's *What's To Be Done*, with its glorification of London's Crystal Palace, which was the glittering monument of the 1852 London Exposition, but which was widely taken as a symbol that the liberal intellectuals were on the right track in their scientific rationalism. Dostoevsky was certain that they were on the wrong track. "Reason is only reason," we hear him saying, "and it satisfies only man's rational requirements," which "amount to perhaps one-twentieth of the whole." "Desire, on the other hand," he observes, "is the manifestation of life itself,—of all of life—and it encompases everything from reason down to scratching oneself. 'Reason' amounts to perhaps one-twentieth of the whole," and because of man's "chronic perversity, desire usually stubbornly disagrees with reason." Man's insistence on the right to be perverse, to yield to whim, to value his free will above all else, however wild and perverse it may be, is man's "greatest advantage", and "causes every system and every theory to crumble into dust on contact."

So much, then, for the 19th-century intellectual establishment. *Notes from the Underground*, as we have it, is not overtly Christian, but it may well have been intended to be overtly Christian if credence can be given to the little-noticed and somewhat mysterious letter from Dostoevsky to his brother Michael, dated March 26, 1864, in which he complained about the passages cut from the work when it was first published. "These swinish censors," he wrote, "left out the passages where I railed at everything and *pretended* to blaspheme; but they deleted the passages where I deduced from all this *the necessity of faith and Christ*." (Italics Dostoevsky's).

In any case "the necessity of faith and Christ" is apparent enough in *Crime and Punishment*, which was published a year-and-a-half later and in which Raskolnikov performed an act of perfect faith in confessing to the murder of the old pawnbroker and her sister when there was no earthly need to confess. We are given to understand that the truth lies in Sonya's Bible and not in Raskolnikov's head, which invented the rationale, based on an atheistic premise, for the act of murder.

In most of Dostoevsky's subsequent works, both major and minor, he perfected and tightened up his dialectic against the intellectual mainstream of his century. He attacked the idea of the natural goodness of man most directly in *The Idiot* by contrasting the members of St. Petersburg society (and hence all society, indeed all mankind) with a truly Christlike figure, Prince Myshkin, in order to demonstrate how weak and wicked the mass of mankind really are. In *The Possessed* he warned the world about the ruthless destruction that is sure to follow when men are ruled by an atheistic government. And in his masterpiece of masterpieces, *The Brothers Karamazov*, his dialectic in favor of faith became so compelling that no atheistic intellectual can deal with it except with fear and trembling. One had to have the intellectual gifts of Ivan Karamazov to understand fully that "If there is no immortality there is no virtue and all is lawful." And Ivan, even after making out as strong a case against Christianity as has ever been made in his "Legend of the Grand Inquisitor," finally ends up like Raskolnikov in performing an act of perfect faith by confessing to a murder when there was no *earthly* reason to confess.

Father Paissey speaks for Dostoevsky when he gives spiritual advice to Alyosha Karamazov and in the process addresses the problem of the intellectuals' effort to exalt science and destroy Christianity:

> Remember, young man, unceasingly, that the science of this world, which has become a great power, has, especially in the last century, analyzed everything divine handed down to us in the holy books. After this cruel analysis the learned of this world have nothing left of all that was sacred of old. But they have only analyzed the parts and overlooked the whole, and indeed their blindness is marvelous. Yet the whole still stands steadfast before their eyes, and the gates of hell shall not prevail against it. Has it not lasted nineteen centuries, is it not still a living, a moving power in the individual soul and in the masses of people? It is still as strong and living even in the souls of atheists, who have destroyed everything! For even those who have renounced Christianity and attack it, in their inmost being still follow the Christian idea, for hitherto neither their subtlety nor the ardor of their hearts has been able to create a higher ideal of man and of virtue than the ideal given by Christ of old.

If ever a man deserved the epithet "Defender of the Faith," it was Dostoevsky, for he lived and wrote at a time when faith was under siege as it had never been before.

But this chapter must not be allowed to end with an account of the beliefs and arguments of Christian thinkers lest it be thought that the influence of Christian intellectuals in the 19th century was more greater than it was. Indeed, Newman was almost drowned in a sea of anti-Christian writings in England, and Kierkegaard and Dostoevsky wrote in languages so foreign to the intellectuals of Western Europe that their strongest influence had to wait until the 20th century. In fact, Kierkegaard was either ignored or dismissed by the 19th century as an eccentric, deformed in mind as well as in body. But he was salvaged by the 20th century and is recognized as a world figure who is far more intellectually troubling to our century than he was to his own because of his compelling case for Christianity. The same is true of Dostoevsky after his works were translated into Western European languages and after the depths of his commitment to Christianity finally came to be understood.

As a parting shot against religion in the 19th century Germany produced the greatest of all the European anti-theists, Friedrich Nietzsche. Nietzsche's anti-theism came to him early and was not, as he himself explained, a consequence of something that had befallen him, but rather was "a matter of instinct." He even dreamed of marshalling the anti-theistic forces of Europe into an organized movement. "There are now," he wrote, "perhaps ten or twenty million men among the different peoples of Europe who no longer believe in God. Is it asking too much that they should get in touch with one another?"

Nietzsche attacked religion generously in many of his works, but his most concentrated effort resulted in *The Anti-Christ*, in which he assures his readers that "Christianity has been the greatest misfortune of mankind so far." Christianity, he concluded, has thrived chiefly because it satisfies man's sadistic and masochistic requirements, the desire to punish and to be punished; furthermore it does not merely fulfill these desires, it creates them. "We immoralists," he says in *The Twilight of the Idols*, "are trying with all our strength to take the concept of guilt and the concept of punishment out of the world again," and the only way the world can be redeemed is to "deny God," to "deny the responsibility of God."

Nietzsche's optimism stemmed chiefly from his vision of what the world could be without religion. "Hearing that the old God is dead," he wrote in *The Joyful Science*

> ... we feel ourselves illumined as by a new dawn. Our hearts overflow with gratitude, surprise, foreknowledge and suspense. ... Now at last the horizon, even if it is not clear, is free once more; now at last our ships can weigh anchor and sail to meet the danger; now once more the pioneer of knowledge has license to attempt whatever he will: the whole expanse of the seas, *our* sea, is accessible to us once more. Never before, perhaps, was there such an open sea.

Thus freed from the tyranny of God, men are free also to pursue their desire for greatness, their will to power, and thereby to demonstrate their own divinity far more satisfactorily than when they were under allegiance to Christianity.

And yet what distinguishes Nietzsche perhaps more sharply from the other anti-theists of his century is his sensitivity to the consequences for Western civilization in giving up God. He was quite aware that Christianity had been the very foundation of Western civilization for almost two thousand years. What will happen when men suddenly find themselves alone with no one to tell them what to do or not do except other men? Nietzsche understood that his announcement of the death of God did not mean an unalloyed triumph for civilization. He could scarcely understand the ease with which unthoughtful thinkers could declare that God did not exist and their expectation that life in an atheistic society would inevitably be better. In his more reflective moments, and there were many of them, he saw that the seas, onto which the ships he spoke of were to be launched, were uncharted and perhaps dark as well. They were not the seas under fair skies with the port in sight, such as his atheistic fellow-intellectuals dreamed of.

Nietzsche got around the possibility of a gloomy future without God by assuming a forced optimism. "There never was a greater event", he declared, than the death of God and we ourselves "have to become Gods to be worthy of it." And so he gambled with the hope that men are good enough to get along without God. He rose like Satan from the floor of Hell to challenge God by becoming a god himself in constructing a theory of the superman in which God is chief adversary.

The skeletal survey in these last two chapters cannot of course begin to do justice to the complexity of the de-Christianizing of the intellectuals of 18th- and 19th-century Europe. It will do little more than suggest the increasing confidence, if not arrogance, among the leading thinkers that men can indeed get along without God to the point that belief in God, and particularly in a Christian God, was no longer even to be entertained. And yet the more the case against Christianity gained momentum, the more powerful, indeed telling, were the arguments of the outnumbered Christian intellectuals, like Newman, Kierkegaard, Dostoevsky, and even

Tolstoy. They perceived that the intellectuals of the 19th century who had liberated themselves from religion had at the same time shackled themselves with premises and attitudes which ignored perhaps 90 percent of what made human nature human.

After a brief look at the corresponding de-Christianizing of the intellectuals in America in the next chapter, this study will continue in the two following chapters to describe the Great Debate as it appears in our own century.

CHAPTER VI

THE DE-CHRISTIANIZING OF AMERICAN INTELLECTUALS

By the time America was able to develop an intellectual life of its own, Christianity in Europe was already under attack, and it was inevitable that American intellectuals would soon be influenced by European intellectuals. As a result, Christian intellectuals dominated American intellectual history for only a short time before giving way to the same anti-Christian forces that dominated Europe.

It is perhaps not sufficiently recognized that the religious zeal which the Pilgrims brought to American shores was short-lived. No one who reads William Bradford's *History of Plymouth Plantation* or Samuel Sewall's *Diary* or any of the other early accounts of the early years in New England can help being impressed with the supreme intensity of religious faith which enabled them not only to seek a new land in which they might freely exercise that faith, but to undergo vast deprivation and suffering from the harshness of their existence once they had found it. And that faith continued strong even after they had managed to make life not only tolerable, but attractive.

Their faith, however, carried with it the seeds of its own destruction, for the doctrine of predestination—which was at the heart of much Calvinist thought—was a doctrine with which men could not live for long. Gradually it was to lose its appeal in America just as it had done in Europe. By 1680, only a little more than half a century later, much of the original theological strength of the Pilgrims had been lost. Their admirable zeal could not compensate adequately for the unworkable theology to which they had committed themselves, so that in time both their zeal and their theology entered into a decline. By the time the third generation of New England Calvinists appeared, the theology of Calvin was already in crisis, and the Protestant faith itself was in jeopardy.

Calvinist clergymen of 17th-century America maintained a solid tradition of intellectualism, and almost all of them were highly educated men. Their education of course had its roots in European thought, for America was far too young to develop any body of thought that could be said to be its own. Virtually all the major ideas of the intellectuals of 17th-century America and much of the 18th century were thus of European origin. The clergy of early New England, having been trained as intellectuals, were naturally eager to know what the current religo-philsoophical doctrines were in Europe, to study them, and to mull them over. As a result, there appeared as early as the end of the 17th century a new breed of young clergymen, who, to be sure, had been well-grounded in Calvinism, but who were also well-grounded in current European philosophical thought—especially that of such contemporaneous English thinkers as Bacon, Hobbes, Locke and the rationalists and deists who followed in Locke's wake. The impact of English empirical thinkers upon the thought of New England clergymen was not dramatic, but it was perhaps less gradual than one might suspect. The fact is that by the middle of the 18th century, the religious zeal of

Protestant clergymen in America had fallen off alarmingly. Henry Bamford Parks in *The American People* observes that "Among the ministers of the early 18th century, if one can judge by the surviving diaries and autobiographies, the sense of sin almost disappeared." And Richard Hofstadter in his book *Anti-Intellectualism in American Life* describes the process as follows:

> By the 1730's and 1740's, the Congregational churches of New England (and often the Presbyterian churches of the Middle Colonies and elsewhere) had lost much of their pristine morals and had settled into dull repositories of the correct faith of the established classes. Abstract and highly intellectual in their traditions, they had lost the power to grip simple people; the Reformation controversies out of which the doctrinal commitments of these churches had grown had lost much of their meaning. The zealots of the first Puritan generation and their well-schooled sons had long since gone to their graves. The ministers themselves had lost much of the drive and therefore the prestige of earlier days. They were highly civilized, often versatile men; but they were in some cases too civilized, too versatile, too worldly, to play anything like their original role.

The Great Awakening, which took place during these years under the inspired leadership of Jonathan Edwards and George Whitefield, is more than anything else a reminder of the low spiritual state into which America had fallen little more than a hundred years after the landing at Plymouth. In a sense, the period of the Great Awakening was the last gasp of Calvinistic theology in America. Edwards and Whitefield exhorted the people to virtue with some of the richest oratory that America had yet heard. In his essay "The Insufficiency of Reason as a Substitute for Revelation," for example, Edwards pointed out that in all our thinking we are driven back to premises which cannot be demonstrated by reason alone, and in *The Great Christian Doctrine of*

Original Sin Defended he argued eloquently against the claims of the rationalists and deists, who discounted or repudiated entirely the doctrine of Original Sin, without which Edwards well knew Christianity would collapse. In his treatise on the *Freedom of the Will* he defended the doctrine of predestination which the encroachments of Arminianism had all but destroyed, but which he regarded rightly as the keystone of Calvinism.

But in the end it was futile for the leaders of the Great Awakening to urge their congregations to repent when the theology which was being urged clearly held that it did no good to repent. Edwards's system, like the deacon's one-horse shay, simply collapsed. Furthermore, among American intellectuals generally (including those among the clergy), the forces of rationalism and deism were already too firmly established to give way before any of the basic Christian doctrines. If they were reading Edwards's religious treatises defending Calvinism, they were also reading Shaftesbury, Hartley, Hutcheson, Hume, Adam Smith, Ferguson and other rationalists and deists who were busy undercutting all religion. Edwards himself once attacked Harvard and Yale for failing to be "nurseries of piety" and for taking more pains "to teaching the scholars human learning than to educate them in religion."

The secularization of Harvard University, in fact, illustrates very well how theology played an ever-decreasing role in the thinking of American intellectuals in the 18th century and after, and how as a result, American intellectuals were transformed from Calvinists into deists and rationalists themselves. At its inception Harvard maintained theology as the center of its curriculum, so that the most influential intellectuals in America were indeed theologically oriented. But in time, theology was taken out of the curriculum and a separate theological school was established, so that in effect those attending other schools at Harvard need not be restricted in their thinking by theological considerations. Such a separation did much to contribute to the rise of secularism in America and to the de-Christianizing of American intellectuals, as non-religious or anti-religious Harvard graduates began to make their influence felt in American intellectual life.

Something of an overall view of the deterioration of the influence of Christianity and the way in which the view of the moral nature of man among American intellectuals passed from the Christian view to the view of the deists and the atheists may be suggested by a catalogue of 17th, 18th, and 19th century American philosophers, all of whom have been substantial contributors to the history of American thought. General agreement on such a catalogue would not be possible, but a sampling of the best histories of American philosophy would lead to a compilation something like this: Jonathan Edwards, Samuel Johnson, John Woolman, Benjamin Franklin, Thomas Jefferson, Elihu Palmer, Ethan Allen, Thomas Paine, John Witherspoon, William Ellery Channing, Theodore Parker, Ralph Waldo Emerson, Henry David Thoreau, Walt Whitman, Simon Newcomb, Noah Porter, James Freeman Clarke, James McCosh, John Fiske, William T. Harris, Josiah Royce, George H. Howison, and Borden Parker Bowne.

If some or many of these names seem obscure, it is largely because early American philosophy itself was obscure. With the exception of two or three philosophers, most notably Jonathan Edwards and perhaps Tom Paine, none of them have enjoyed any considerable influence abroad, and none with the exception of Edwards and perhaps Royce can claim anything like a thorough philosophical system at all comparable to that of the major European philosophers of the same historical periods. Others are not even primarily philosophers, though like Thoreau and Whitman, their philosophical influence has been great. Surely America will be forgiven its generally undistinguished contribution to philosophy, especially in the 18th and 19th centuries, for the exigencies of its newness and its history have, until fairly recently, prevented American intellectuals from becoming professional philosophers.

But the intention of this catalogue is not to point up the feebleness of philosophical thought in this country; but rather to indicate how thoroughly anti-Christian most of it is, or at least how non-Christian. To be sure, the philosophical systems of Edwards, Johnson, Woolman, and Witherspoon are thoroughly Christian-oriented, though only Edwards comes close to orthodox Calvinism. In general, these men represent the vain endeavor to keep the early New England religious enthusiasm alive in the 18th century; but how badly they lost out is suggested by the fact that virtually every other thinker in this catalogue has either repudiated most of the basic doctrines of Christianity outright, or is basically atheistic in his thinking.

Franklin, Jefferson, Palmer, Allen, and Paine were all thoroughgoing deists in the European tradition, and as such tended to deny the divinity of Christ and hence all the doctrines which stem from it. Rather they generally espoused the doctrine of the natural goodness of man as did their European brethren. The transcendentalists, which included Channing, Parker, Emerson, Thoreau, Peirce, and by extension Whitman, represent in general a more advanced stage of the growth of the idea of the natural goodness of man and hence a step even farther removed from traditional Christianity. The evolutionists, like Newcomb, Porter, Clark, McCosh, and Fiske represent early steps toward the rise of atheism in America under the influence of Darwinism, which tended to reduce the traditional gap between men and beasts to an embarrassing minimum. The new dignity which these philosophers assigned to the scientific method constituted a firm implantation of the Comtean spirit in America. The pragmatism of Peirce, James, and Dewey forbade their admitting Christianity into their system, and Dewey, as we shall see, was a thoroughgoing atheist.

It would not be accurate to say that the majority of the Founding Fathers were anti-Christian or that they were even deists. Most of the framers of the Constitution, in fact, were Episcopalians; some were Congregationalists, Presbyterians, Quakers, Methodists, Baptists, and even Catholics. Only a few were deists or Unitarians. None were professed atheists. But it is symptomatic of the decline of religion among American intellectuals that three of the most influential fathers of our country—Franklin, Jefferson, and Paine—were deists, and in fact subscribed to none of the doctrines connected with the divinity of Christ. Jefferson himself was lambasted liberally by the clergy for his free-thinking and his repudiation of basic Christian doctrines. Concerning Calvin himself, his reaction was extremely violent. "If ever man worshipped a false God, he did," said Jefferson in a letter to John Adams. "It would be more pardonable to believe in no God at all than to blaspheme him by the atrocities of Calvin." And yet these observations typify to a degree the deist view of basic Calvinist doctrine.

In a sense Jefferson carried on his own private war against religion in general and Christianity in particular.

He was instrumental, for example, in abolishing the professorships of Hebrew, of theology, and of ancient languages at William and Mary College. In his early life he lost faith in the Bible by applying merely historical tests to it, and in later life he tried his hand at the "higher criticism" of the Bible—the kind that was to destroy its authority in Europe. Nor can there be any doubt that his crusade for religious freedom, as admirable as it was, stemmed primarily from the fact that he could not stomach fundamental Christian doctrines.

Something of the tenor of Jefferson's own philosophical position is suggested by his admiration of Epicurus and Epictetus, men whose thought was essentially incompatible with religion, and his repudiation of Plato, whose thought was not. Like the deists generally, Jefferson was inclined toward the doctrine of the natural goodness of man. Jefferson was simply too much an intellectual of his time, and too profoundly influenced by the current anti-Christian philosophical thought of Europe to be very Christian in his outlook.

Benjamin Franklin's thinking and writing are no more a celebration of Christian doctrine than Jefferson's. Like many other deists he, too, believed in God and in the immortality of the soul, and he even believed in some kind of heaven and hell. In fact, in one of Franklin's most thoughtful moments he asked of Tom Paine, "If man are so wicked with religion, what would they be without it?" But there is nothing specifically Christian about Franklin's beliefs, despite the fact that he was a professional moralist.

Alongside Tom Paine's, however, Franklin's religious thought seemed reactionary. Paine's *Age of Reason* was one of the most widely-read and influential anti-religious treatises of all time. "I do not believe", he says, "in the creed professed by the Jewish Church, by the Roman Church, by the Greek Church, by the Protestant Church, nor by any other Church that I know of. My own mind is my own church." Despite the widely acknowledged shallowness of Paine's thought in *The Age of Reason*, his sophomoric literalness in interpreting the Bible, his exuberant disrespect for tradition, and his adolescent sneers at all fundamental religious doctrines, the widespread popularity of this famous anti-Christian tract demonstrates how early in American history American intellectuals were disposed to unbelief.

But other, if less famous, thinkers were also at work in America. Shortly after the Revolutionary War, for example, Elihu Palmer, who was an ardent disciple of Rousseau and who was therefore declared a heretic by the Baptists (to whose church he once belonged), helped set up a "Deistical Society" in New York, which, among other things, was designed to clear the air of "superstition and fanaticism," i.e., orthodox Christianity—and to establish a "genuine natural morality" based on the natural goodness of man. Ethan Allen, another 18th-century American philosopher, also rejected the authority of Revelation and espoused the increasingly popular view that men in their natural state are so good that they do not need a personal God.

This shift from Calvinism to Rousseauism in America did not, it must be emphasized again, occur spontaneously. In fact, it occurred through what might be called the de-evolution of Christian theology, the chief intermediate step of which was Unitarianism. Vernon L. Parrington described the process as follows: "Changing its name and arraying itself in garments cut after the best Yankee fashion, the gospel of Jean Jacques Rousseau presently walked the streets of Boston, and spoke from its most respectable pulpits under the guise of Unitarianism." The word *respectable* is important here, for the gospel of Rousseau was preached most forcefully and most eloquently by two of the most respectable intellectuals in America, Channing and Emerson. Both were of the Unitarian persuasion, although Emerson in time found that he could not even stay with the Unitarians.

Whereas the Calvinists had widened the gap between man and God about as far as it could be widened, the Transcendentalists so far closed the gap that man and God actually touched, even to the point of producing a pantheistic view of the universe, a development particularly pronounced in the thinking of Emerson. No consideration was given to the traditional Catholic view that kept God at a safe distance from man while at the same time it kept open the lines of communication. Catholicism had virtually no influence on American intellectuals in the 19th century. Except for Orestes Brownson and one or two others, there were no American Catholic intellectuals. The alternative was a simple either/or proposition: Either man was totally depraved, as Calvin held, or he was totally good, as Emerson held. Philosophers and intellectuals both in England and America had, for more than a century, been preparing the way for the triumph of the idea of the natural goodness of man and the destruction of the Calvinistic doctrine of total depravity.

Quite understandably and quite admirably the transcendentalists were reacting against the authority of science and materialistic philosophical systems which had been building up throughout the 18th century under the guise of an idealism which seemed on the surface to reaffirm man's spiritual nature rather than deny it. But they drew their inspiration from the German idealists, and they, too, abandoned those basic doctrines without which Christianity loses its meaning.

It was William Ellery Channing, the founder of Unitarianism, who perhaps most effectually proclaimed the new era of sinlessness in America. Channing had emancipated himself from both Calvinism and Christianity while he was yet a young man—chiefly under the spell of Jefferson and Rousseau. In 1819 he proclaimed in a famous sermon his new gospel of "Unitarian Christianity," which cannot be considered Christianity at all, but which officially announces his shift from Calvinism to Rousseauism in his depreciation of the doctrine of Original Sin. This sermon was highly influential, and Channing's thinking contributed immensely to the rise of the idea in America of man's inherent sinlessness, and hence to the idea of the Indiscriminate God as opposed to the Arbitrary God of Calvinism or the Merciful but Just God of traditional Christianity.

Yet Channing's thought was only a tentative step along the way to the full-blown Romanticism of Emerson, for Channing maintained a certain respect for Revelation, and he insisted upon the superiority of unaided reason over the emotions as a guide to right moral behavior. Emerson, on the other hand, pursued the idea of the natural goodness of man to its logical conclusion by asserting that man's truest guide lay in his impulses and instincts and that it was they rather than reason or Relevation that men should follow. Emerson began under the influence of Channing, but his thinking led him to break away not only from Christianity but from Channing and the Unitarians as well. Emerson's thought was profoundly anti-rational and anti-Christian. By relying on the intuitive faculty, Emerson felt certain that men could not only be like gods, but indeed be gods. For having rejected the doctrine of Original Sin, he was able to conclude that in fact God and man and nature are all one. Randall Stewart in his study of *American Literature and Christian Doctrine* is exaggerating very little perhaps when he summarizes Emerson's thought and influence by observing: "By no dint of sophistry can he be brought into the Christian fold. His doctrine is radically anti-Christian, and has done more than any other doctrine to undermine Christian belief in America."

If there was any man who had a more profound unawareness of sin than Emerson it was perhaps another famous American, Walt Whitman, whose mind was saturated with Emerson's thought, as he himself readily acknowledged. Whitman, however, did not inherit the highly developed New England moral conscience which was Emerson's, so that he was more nearly free to practice what Emerson preached, as a study of his life will testify. In a sense, Whitman is the "compleat pagan," wholly free from the strictures of Christian doctrine or from any theological considerations whatsoever. The resulting lack of humility is suggested by the fact that words like "egotism" and "arrogance" have no pejorative meaning in Whitman's vocabulary. "I dote upon myself," he says in *Son of Myself*. "There is that lot of me and all so luscious. Nothing, not God, is greater to one than one's self is. Nor do I understand who there can be more wonderful than myself."

Like many another patriotic American, Whitman seemed to believe that the doctrine of Original Sin was somehow un-American. It was almost too much to contemplate that in this land of the free everyone had to begin the race for the good life with so major a moral handicap. In the 18th and 19th centuries especially, the despair which the doctrine of total depravity engendered in those who felt sinful ran counter to the indomitable optimism of the pioneers. Europeans perhaps were tainted with Original Sin, but not Americans.

The early American idealists, thinkers like William T. Harris, Josiah Royce, Borden Bowne, and George Howison, shared the transcendentalists' abhorrence of materialism and scientism; but in adopting the doctrines of Kant, and especially Hegel, they cannot be said to have done much to perpetuate the Christian view of man, either in the tradition of Calvin or in the tradition of Catholicism.

Yet, however little the transcendentalists and the American idealists contributed to the perpetuation of Christianity, they recognized the spiritual nature of man and were fully aware of the moral dangers of materialist and positivist philosophical systems. But in time they were to be overwhelmed by the materialists and the positivists whom they abhorred and who got their first solid foothold in America from Darwin's evolutionism.

The theory of evolution had an enormous impact on American thought just as it did on European thought. American theologians tended to regard it as a serious blow to Christianity because it appeared to invalidate the Christian view not only of the origin of man, but indeed his very nature, including above all his moral and spiritual nature. Most American philosophers, on the other hand, took an optimistic view of the theory by interpreting it as further evidence of God's grand design. Those who felt that evolution threatened religious faith felt especially that it had undermined the Book of Genesis, including the account of Original Sin therein described. Some even held that the theory implied that man was no more a moral creature than any of the other creatures who struggle for survival, in which case the doctrine of Original Sin was rendered meaningless. But those who welcomed the theory of evolution in America tended to be cheerful about man's moral nature. As a result they ignored the importance of the doctrine of Original Sin to Christianity and proposed a moral evolution of man comparable to the anatomical evolution which Darwin described. Many even thought they saw signs of man's moral improvement in the 19th century over the preceding century, and some tended to believe that men might in time wholly outgrow their original sinfulness.

But perhaps the most important effect of the theory of evolution was that it gave far greater dignity to the scientific method than it had hitherto enjoyed in America. It encouraged the application of the scientific method to evaluate the moral behavior as well as the physical evolution of men, and not only to further depreciate the traditional Christian view of man but indeed to discredit the authority of all religion. Thus the seeds of scientific rationalism were firmly planted on American soil.

This brief sketch of the de-Christianizing of certain key figures in the intellectual history of America will suggest that American thought was at all times heavily dependent upon that of Europe. The early American settlers looked almost wholly to European Calvinists for their doctrines and their inspiration. The first indigenous American philosopher was Jonathan Edwards, and even his thought owes much to European thinkers, including Locke and Newton. The American deists owed almost all their ideas to European deists, and the transcendentalists owed most to German philosophers such as Schelling.

The American philosophical idealists were heavily indebted to the post-Kantian philosophers and the American evolutionists were heavily indebted to Darwin and Spencer. Thus, American philosophical thought was never far behind European thought in adopting views that were hostile to Christianity. As the next chapter will suggest, where American thought in the 20th century has been most original, it has also been most anti-Christian.

CHAPTER VII

SOLIDIFYING THE POST-CHRISTIAN AGE

The course of intellectual history in the 20th century has been in the direction of spreading and hardening the atheism of 18th- and 19th-century thought to the point that among the vast majority of intellectuals now, the idea that there is no God, at least no personal God, is axiomatic.

Nietzsche lingered on into 1900 as if to make certain that Western intellectual history entered the 20th century with a full recognition that God is indeed dead and that henceforth men are going to have to shift for themselves. And yet even in the early 20th century there were intellectuals who felt that God was not quite as dead as He ought to be, and they thus contributed their bit to administering the *coup de grace*. Among the most notable of these was Sigmund Freud, the most influential mind of the early 20th century. Freud and Nietzsche were in hearty agreement that psychology and science are man's best friends and that religion is his worst enemy. Release from religion, they were certain, was the only sure way to happiness, for it meant freedom from guilt, from neuroses, from crippling inhibitions. The eradication of religion could thus lead to contentment, creativeness, pleasure, and power. Both thinkers felt that religion developed to fill basic psychological needs, but that ultimately it produced more pain than pleasure, as well as dangerous illusions which lead men away from the truth rather than toward it.

Freud, however, had no illusions about the goodness of man's moral nature; on the contrary, he was convinced that men are driven by a complex of dark desires which can, if not checked, lead them to their destruction or to the destruction of others. But unlike Calvin and Luther, who match him in their dim view of natural man, he recognized no saving grace conferred by God. On the contrary, he was even more relentless than Nietzsche in pursuing his anti-theistic position, and in a series of works, including *Totem and Taboo*, *Moses and Mono-Theism*, and *The Future of an Illusion*, he applied his psychoanalytic theories to demonstrate that religion is merely a product of wish-fullfillment, that it perpetuates infantile behavior patterns, and that it is a particularly dangerous form of illusion because it impedes the efforts of the scientific method to find out the real truth about the human condition and how to improve it. Thus, if Freud had no faith in religion or in reason as the proper means to truth, he still had faith in science, however unscientific his own conclusions about man's nature may have been. As Freudianism spread westward, it carried with it Freud's anti-theistic premise. Eventually it came to permeate American culture more completely than any other.

After Freud, the most exciting and perhaps the most influential way of looking at man's condition and destiny by 20th century European intellectuals is the way of the existentialists. For the purposes of this study, it is necessary to distinguish two fundamental branches of existentialists: Christian existentialists and atheistic existentialists. Whatever the existentialists have in common that enables them all to be called existentialists, the fact remains that Christian existentialists like Kierkegaard and Gabriel Marcel are so far removed in their thinking from unbelieving existentialists like Heidegger and Sartre and Merleau-Ponty that their similarities become relatively inconsequential. The overriding difference is that the unbelieving existentialists insist on the supremacy of man. The Christian existentialists, having perceived that reason and science will never provide adequate answers to the eternal questions, also perceive that the answers, if they can be found at all, must be found in religion, specifically Christianity. The atheist existentialists, on the other hand, also punctured the puny life raft of reason-and-science which had kept the atheist (and deist) intellectuals of the 18th and 19th centuries afloat. But more important, they also rejected the authority of religion and Revelation and hence any supra-human source of morality; so that whereas the Christian existentialists proposed a kind of neo-fideism, the atheist existentialists became more heavily dependent than ever upon their atheism; and instead of making their exit by way of religion, they concluded that in this world there is no exit.

Furthermore, the atheist existentialists have so far beat out their believing brethren that the phrase "atheistic existentialism" has become almost a tautology. It turns out that after Kierkegaard, the works of believing existentialists such as Maritain and Karl Barth, who will be discussed in the next chapter, were merely minor setbacks in the onward march of unbelieving existentialists from Heidegger to Sartre and beyond.

German existentialism, particularly in the hands of its two leading representatives, Martin Heidegger and

Karl Jaspers, does not take a militantly anti-Christian stance. It is true that both thinkers are widely considered to be atheists, and although both have rejected the charge, it is not too much to say that they have done nothing for Christianity and in fact the spirit of Heidegger leans heavily on much modern atheistic thinking, including the death-of-God theologians.

Heidegger was raised a Catholic and was even a novice among the Jesuits, but his thinking led him out of the Christian framework, past the neo-Kantians and into the orbit of Edmund Husserl, the founder of phenomonology. In time he developed a full philosophical system of his own with a solidly existential foundation. His phenomenological orientation led him to reject all theories of truth based on Christian theology or indeed on any supernatural explanation of truth. Heidegger's preoccupation with nihilism has strong anti-Christian overtones and the core of his philosophical thought more nearly resembles Kant's and even Nietzsche's than Kierkegaard's. Basically he seems to have concluded that pure reflective thought cannot attain to the assertion of God. Perhaps one of the reasons scholars have so much difficulty in defining Heidegger's attitude toward religion is that, having concluded that God does not fall within the province of human thought, Heidegger cannot find Him within the province of man.

Like Heidegger, and indeed like most of the influential philosophers since Descartes, Karl Jaspers did not launch his search for the truth from premises in the Bible or elsewhere in the Christian tradition. Like them, he established his own premises, and then determined where and if God and Christianity fit into his own personal scheme. Whether He fits or doesn't fit, Jaspers often talks about God, but he doesn't really say much about Him.

At one point he reduces God to a nonentity: "God is only a name," he says; but, like Heidegger, he considers the idea of God not to be a possible subject for human thought. "The One God eludes thought," he writes, "and is unthinkable; if He could be thought about, He would be a finite among other finites." "And so," he concludes, "God is remote and incomprehensible, so remote as to seem unallowable, so incomprehensible as to seem to vanish into nothingness." Jaspers seems to inhabit a limbo somewhere between Kierkegaard and Nietzsche, but those who think of him as an atheist may be more nearly right. Even his most sympathetic interpreter, Paul Ricoeur, admits that Jaspers's thought resolves itself into an "inchoate atheism." In any case it is difficult to think of either Heidegger or Jaspers as friends of religion in general and Christianity in particular, and certainly their influence has been in the direction of turning attention away from Christianity rather than toward it.

But if there is any ambiguity at all on the part of German existentialists on the subject of Christianity, the anti-theism of the French atheistic existentialists is unmistakable. At the same time, the French atheist existentialists developed a far greater sense of the loss of God, and what that loss meant philosophically and psychologically, than either Heidegger or Jaspers. Among those who have registered perhaps the greatest sensitivity to the problem of living in a Godless world were Sartre and Camus, for they were able to express their anguish in the form of plays and novels as well as philosophical essays. It is true that Sartre explains in *The Words* that he was only a boy when he lost his faith in God, Who "tumbled into the blue and disappeared," and that he never suffered "the slightest temptation to bring Him back to life." But his *Nausea* nonetheless affords one of the 20th-century's most powerful descriptions of what life should be like to the true unbeliever. "Here we sit," says Roquentin, "all of us, eating and drinking to preserve our precious existence and really there is nothing, nothing, absolutely no reason for existing." *Nausea* is an exquisite portrayal of the ultimate futility of all human actions and aspirations and efforts in a Godless world as Roquentin experiences the stench of life at every turn. It is true that the uncomfortable atheism of Sartre's earlier years became increasingly comfortable as he transferred his attention more and more away from the problem of the individual in a meaningless world to a dialectical sociology in which he tried to find a meaning in life where he previously had found none. The key concept in his view is *engagement*, commitment, but he also insists that there are bad commitments as well as good commitments, and he could never solve the problem of what the criterion should be.

On balance it may be that Camus has communicated a greater sensitivity and understanding of the problems attending unbelief than Sartre, or indeed any other 20th-century writer. His famous statement in *The Myth of Sisyphus* that the only really serious philosophical problem is the problem of suicide suggests something of this understanding. Camus ultimately comes out against suicide, though not on very convincing grounds. "Make known to us the truth about this world—which is that it has none," Caesonia intones in *Caligula*, "and grant us strength to live up to this verity of verities."

Camus and Sartre, at least early in their careers, were quite aware of the limited goodness of human nature, but when they perceived how intolerable life is for bad men without a good God, they were forced to reevaluate man's moral nature upward in order to justify their righteous indignation over the injustices of the world, and thus to hold out some hope for human survival. Sartre was to argue that existentialism is a humanism after all, and hence to argue that men are better than he previously had thought. Dr. Rieux at the end of *The Plague* concludes—with Camus himself—that "there is more in men to admire than to despise." Both Camus and Sartre had talked themselves into some faint hope that man can somehow make it without God after all. The appeal to human fraternity was Camus' ultimate appeal, but it was human fraternity without God.

Another modern French thinker whose influence puts him in the front ranks of anti-theistic intellectuals is Maurice Merleau-Ponty, who in his youth knew the Catholic faith well and believed in it and who, before his violent and untimely death, asked for (and later got) a Christian burial. In between, however, his thinking took him so far away from Christianity that he came to regard the very idea of God as a humiliation to man because it reduced him to slavery. "I think that it is naturally inherent for man to think of God," he admitted once, "This, however, does not mean that He exists." He became firmly convinced that under God's scrutiny man was stripped of his powers, including, above all, his freedom, and he could not endure the thought. He found that life is not only embarrassing under the eye of God, but intolerable, and he would have none of Him. Christianity he found to be particularly stifling, as if the plot of a man's life were already given away, and thus the mystery was spoiled for him. The phrase "Thy will be done" epitomized God as a master manipulator.

Though Merleau-Ponty was deep in the existentialist tradition, he found the concept of a "Christian existentialist" to be a contradiction in terms, despite thinkers like Kierkegaard and Gabriel Marcel, and he could quite understand Pope Pius XII's condemnation of existentialism. Before Merleau-Ponty was done, or rather, before he was killed, he had attacked Christianity from almost every vantage point—philosophically, historically, and ethically—and his thinking has left a distinct mark on the 20th-century history of ideas.

The influence of the anti-scientific bent of atheistic existentialism did not prevent scientists from converting to anti-Christian thought. In fact, the influence of the scientific spirit on philosophy has been far greater in the 20th century than in the 19th, and, as we shall see, may have destroyed it utterly. Alfred North Whitehead was the first 20th-century philosopher to attempt a full-blown philosophical system which took a scientific cosmology into account. Actually, as his interests turned from mathematics to science and then to metaphysics, he never really lost interest in religion and the problem of God, but he ultimately ended up with a natural theology which does not or could not take the doctrines of Christianity into account; and the notion that God spoke to man through the Scriptures, or indeed in any other effective way, had no meaning for him.

Other scientifically-oriented intellectuals in the 20th century, however, were not so deferential to religion as Whitehead was. That spirit of science which attacked the authority of Christianity in the 19th century is perhaps best represented in the 20th century by Julian Huxley, the grandson of Thomas Henry Huxley. Thomas Henry Huxley had begun his life in the Christian faith but after he became a Darwinian he began to deliver devastating attacks against Christianity, including attacks against those who claimed to prove that a supernatural God exists, and especially against those who claimed supernatural authority either for the Bible or for Christian doctrine. Bishop Wilberforce, who was a major spokesman for Christianity at the time, was a particular target of Huxley's, and so was W. E. Gladstone. And in the view of many, Huxley's rhetoric, if not his thinking, left him victorious.

Julian Huxley inherited the biological evolutionary theories of his grandfather and proceeded to develop a theory that biological evolution and cultural evolution are all part of s single process. This position enabled him to be both optimistic and anti-Christian. Man not only didn't need God because he was evolving nicely on his own, but Christianity in fact was hindering the process of evolution, with its emphasis upon sin, both original and unoriginal. Julian Huxley exudes confidence and peace of mind in his relentless attacks on theism in general and Christianity in particular. He took the trouble to write a book called *Religion Without Revelation*, in which he assumed something of the role of a visionary in portraying an ever-evolving world moving toward a "divinization of existence" with the understanding that a new definition of "the divine" would be "free from all connotations of external supernatural beings." "Theistic religions," he insisted, "with their inescapable basis of divine revelations and dogmatic theologies, are today not merely incompatible with human progress and the advance of human knowledge, but are obstacles to the emergence of new types of religion which could be compatible with our knowledge and capable of promoting our future progress."

Strictly speaking, the phrase "theistic religions" is a tautology and the phrase "religion without revelation" ought to be regarded as a contradiction, but like many another anti-theist, Huxley liked to attach a desirable connotation to the term "religion" in a figurative sense even though he repudiated utterly all the premises of all the great religions of the world, and the not-so-great as well. He prefers to think of religion as "applied spiritual ecology," which must contemplate "the relations of mankind with the rest of external nature." He would have no truck with the relationship between man and God, and certainly would not entertain the thought that Christianity or any other revealed religion could enhance the other relationships he speaks of.

But Julian Huxley was a distinguished biologist in his own right, and one of the few outstanding scientists who wrote with a broad knowledge of the humanities. The kind of scientific humanism which he advocated has had a particular appeal to intellectuals in England, Holland, Scandinavia, and especially, as we shall see, in America. They are primarily intellectuals who, like himself, have somehow escaped the anguish and perhaps the awareness of the consequences of the loss of God which afflicted thinkers like Dostoevsky, Kierkegaard, Nietzsche, Camus, and Sartre. Huxley represents the comfortable anti-theist *par excellence*, and as such he may even head the list of major unthoughtful thinkers.

Still another intellectual of high stature whose commitment to scientific rationalism made him an archenemy of Christianity was Bertrand Russell, who was Whitehead's disciple, and who, like Whitenead, was a mathematician as well as a metaphysician. Russell and Whitehead in fact collaborated on one of their principal works, the 3-volume *Principia Mathematica* (1910-1913). But Russell was also much more. He was what one might call a cradle radical. His parents were free-thinkers and encouraged Russell to free-think too. He was expelled from Cambridge for preaching pacifism; he became involved in endless social causes, which occupied him to the very end of his long life. He wrote dozens of books on subjects ranging from government, education and world peace, to sex and religion, and almost all of them were of a radical nature. But even those who don't know him for his writings know him for his participation in social-action causes. In 1935 he was referred to by a German historian as "the only British thinker of the age who enjoys world-wide repute." It is of some consequence, then, that Russell was one of the most outspoken spokesmen against Christianity in the 20th century. Many influential intellectuals in the 20th century who are ardent antitheists have been hesitant to put their religious sentiments in writing. Russell, on the other hand, was always eager to get his into indelible form, and he did so in works ranging from *Religion and Science* and *Human Society in Ethics and Politics*, to an essay entitled "Why I am not a Christian," which has become so well known that it is widely anthologized, even in college freshman textbooks. In fact Russell's views on religion aroused such interest that they became the subject of two books, both entitled *Why Bertrand Russell is Not a Christian*, one in 1928, and the other in 1959.

Russell was nourished on the heritage of the 19th- and 20th-century thought which declared the supremacy of science-and-reason over the authority of religion. Christianity, he insisted, not only spoils sex, but it spoils almost everything else. "I am myself a dissenter from all known religions," he wrote in 1922 in *Skeptical Essays*, "and I hope that every kind of religious belief will die out." Sounding a bit like the 19th-century Comteans, he observes, "I regard religion as belonging to the infancy of human reason and to a stage of development which we are now outgrowing." He insists that Christianity has done far more harm than good, and he is deeply suspicious of the institutional churches of Christianity. He upholds the tyranny of the scientific fact, and he gives no quarter to anyone whose premises are non-scientific.

And yet, unlike Julian Huxley, Russell in his reflections does not see a world of light and joy without God. He recognizes that a godless philosophy is necessarily a gloomy philosophy, and at age 92 he declared that "the secret of happiness is to face the fact that the world is terrible." And even in the process of denying the existence of God he recognizes that at times he is dealing only in probabilities. He was nonetheless one of the great anti-Christian spokesmen in the 20th century, and if his campaign against God is not so unrelenting as Nietzsche's or Freud's was, it was because he had so many other things to do.

In recent years philosophy, especially in the Anglo-Saxon world, has gone a step beyond the thinking of Huxley and Russell. It stepped into linguistic analysis, so that philosophy has now been reduced largely to a matter of analyzing language, not only independently of metaphysics, but in effect as a tool to destroy metaphysics, and indeed any philosophical "system" whatsoever. It is an outgrowth and perhaps an inevitable consequence of the influence of science on philosophical thought. It is a kind of offshoot of logical positivism. Its most famous proponent was Ludwig Wittgenstein, an Anglicized Austrian.

Wittgenstein at first thought of a career in engineering but, like Bertrand Russell, he turned to mathematics and then to philosophy, and, in fact, fell under the influence of Russell and his logic at Cambridge. His subsequent variegated and spectacular career led him to be in turn a hermit, a soldier, a prisoner, and an elementary school teacher, as well as something of a musician and sculptor. At one time he came within an ace of entering a monastery. He published his most important work, *Tractatus Logico-Philosophicus* in 1921. He subsequently returned for six years to Cambridge during which time he delivered a series of lectures so brilliant that his philosophical wake was felt for years afterward. He worked in a London hospital during World War II, and returned to lecture at Cambridge, but concluded that his influence was more bad than good. He resigned and sojourned for varying periods in Ireland, America, and Norway. Finally he returned to Cambridge, where he died of tuberculosis in 1951. During these years, however, he did much thinking, chiefly by way of refining what he had said in the *Tractatus*. The *Tractatus* is less than 80 pages long, but its influence on philosophical thought and hence on subsequent philosophers' views of Christianity (among other things) has been enormous. Wittgenstein drew such a sharp distinction between science and philosophy—in favor of science—that he concluded that only science can properly ask and answer the great questions, and that the role of philosophy is merely to give a precision and clarity to scientific problems and conclusions—hence his concern with the meaning of words and his emphasis on the analysis of language. Given such premises, it is not possible even to talk intelligibly about scientifically unverifiable concepts like God or immortality or ethics. It is absurd even to speak of them, and the mystery of life must forever remain a mystery. "Even where *all possible* scientific questions have been answered," he observed in the *Tractatus*, "the problems of life will remain completely untouched." And neither philosophy nor religion nor any other discipline is allowed to touch them.

Thus analytical and linguistic philosophy in the hands of Wittgenstein and his distinguished disciples, including Rudolph Carnap, Alfred Ayer, and Karl Popper, and indeed a host of others, is not merely anti-religious, it is not even pro-philosophy. Like a heat-seeking missile, it searches out philosophical systems wherever they may be found and destroys them by analyzing their language. Thus, insofar as their influence prevails—and it may now be said to prevail in England, America, Scandinavia, and the Lowlands, as well as in Vienna—it has utterly destroyed the grand tradition of philosophy from Plato, Aristotle, Aquinas, Descartes, Hegel, Kant, even down to Nietzsche himself, because it has destroyed the ability to relate language to fact. It's rather like a piano teacher concluding that there is not now, and never has been, such a thing as a piano. One ironic result is that the threat that philosophy often seemed to pose to religion has now been largely neutralized because Christianity is now no more false than any other system or body of thought. It destroys philosophical systems that are anti-Christian as well as those that are pro-Christian. For an atheist to declare that God does not exist is quite as absurd as for a Christian to declare that He does exist. The real effect of analytical philosophy, however, has clearly been in favor of atheism, not of Christianity.

Thusfar we have been discussing the efforts of 20th century West European intellectuals to solidify the post-Christian age, but similar efforts of Russian and American intellectuals in the 20th century must not be ignored.

The fact that some 400 million people are living in countries which were at one time Christian but which are now officially atheistic is due in remarkable degree to the thinking of a single Russian intellectual, namely Vladmir Ilyitch Lenin. From one end of the Soviet empire to the other Lenin's face gazes from posters and postage stamps and frowns from multi-storied pedestals. Nor is his face unknown in the countries of Eastern Europe. It may be said that he has influenced the thinking and the lives of more people than any figure since the founders of the great religions.

He was of course the philosophical heir of Marx, and Marx considered the destruction of Christianity to be axiomatic in order to achieve a utopian socialist state. But whereas Marx challenged Christianity only in his correspondence and only in private, and then only in theory, Lenin set out to destroy it in real life. Whereas Marx called religion "opium for the people," Lenin vulgarized the expression by turning it into "spiritual bathtub-gin," in which the slaves of capitalism drown their dignity.

Actually Lenin was an atheist long before he knew anything of Marx or Engels, so the atheistic assumptions underlying the philosophies of Marx and Engels caused him no trouble. And, like many intellectuals of his time, he saw science as the key to the development of socialism. "The proletariat of today," he wrote, "takes the side of socialism, which enlists science in the battle against the fog of religion, and frees the workers from their belief in life after death by welding them together to fight in the present for a better life on earth." His anti-theism was of the most beligerent kind, as the following specimen of his thinking suggests: "Marxism is materialism. As such, it is as relentlessly hostile to religion as was the materialism of the 18th-century Encyclopedists or the materialism of Feuerbach. This is beyond doubt. But the dialectical materialism of Marx and Engels goes further than the

Encyclopedists and Feuerbach, for it applies materialistic philosophy to the domain of history, to the domain of the social sciences. We must combat religion—that is the ABC of *all* materialism, and consequently of Marxism. But Marxism is not a materialism which has stopped at the ABCs. Marxism goes further. It says: 'We must know how to combat religion, and in order to do so, we must explain the source of faith and religion among the masses in a *materialist* way.' "

Lenin was pleased to be able to draw upon a tradition of a century-and-a-half of anti-theistic thought in Western Europe to serve the ends of Soviet communism. As a result he had little difficulty in winning over most Russian intellectuals to his crusade to de-Christianize the entire nation, though, as the next chapter will indicate, there later appeared some troublesome non-converts. Nowhere have the labors of 19th-century intellectuals born more abundant and characteristic fruit than in Eastern Europe.

In America, of all the philosophical movements, the most nearly indigenous was pragmatism. In fact pragmatism may be thought of as America's chief contribution to philosophical thought. It was Charles Sanders Peirce who coined the term "pragmatism," but it was William James who perhaps best defined and refined it. The whole function of philosophy ought to be, says James, "to find out what definite difference it will make to you and me, at definite instances of our life, if this world-formula or that world-formula be the true one." The idea of pragmatism is "to try to interpret each notion by tracing its practical consequences."

As America's most distinctive contribution to philosophy, pragmatism cannot be said to have bolstered

Christianity any more than deism or Emersoniansim. In fact, pragmatism is almost by definition anti-religious, for the God of pragmatism is created by man and therefore has behind it a profound cynicism of which it can never quite divest itself. Furthermore, the pragmatist is necessarily a relativist, so that his thinking runs directly counter to the absolute morality of Christianity. It will be clear, for example, that James's method of testing the truth of an idea is attended with some difficulties when applied to certain Christian doctrines. It is not easy to apply the pragmatic test to the redemption, the atonement, grace, and so on, because the dead who believed in them or did not believe in them have not, for the most part, communicated to the living whether their belief or disbelief had any "practical consequences." Ultimately James threw in his lot with God not from any theological argument or from sheer conviction but from primarily psychological consideration, namely that men are happier with religion than without it.

Thus, although James's pragmatism accepted a belief in God, to those with less spiritual sensitivity pragmatism in fact invites atheism. John Dewey was one of those who accepted the invitation. Dewey's influence on modern American thought and indeed on European thought is perhaps greater than any other modern American thinker. In a sense, Dewey's philosophical system is a synthesis of all the major anti-Christian philosophical systems of the late 19th century both in Europe and America. And yet it has a character all its own as is always the case with the products of powerful philosophical minds. In his early career, Dewey was an idealist strongly under the influence of Hegel. He professed a belief in God, in absolute reality, and in a perfect will. But in time, large doses of Locke, Hume, Lamarck,

Huxley, Darwin, Spencer, Peirce, and William James overwhelmed his idealism. By the 1890's he was converted to a materialistic, evolutionistic, relativistic, naturalistic, pragmatic position which made him ultimately a thoroughgoing atheist.

Under the potent influence of Darwin and William James, Dewey adopted an evolutionist and biological approach to nature and the problems of man, and he thus emphasized the fundamental anti-religious view that man is continuous with nature rather than above it, as the religious view holds. All things are to be explained through a study of nature. Man's spiritual nature is denied, his immortality is denied, the validity of Revelation is denied, the authority of the Church is denied, and finally God Himself is denied. "Faith in the Divine Author and authority in which Western Civilization confided," said Dewey, "has been made impossible for the cultivated mind of the Western World." Man has no moral nature except as society assigns him one. Morals become merely social habits, which themselves are ever subject to change. Society, not God or religion, is the proper arbiter of proper behavior. What in one generation is immoral may in the next generation be quite acceptable. Man has no moral sense, and the phenomenon of conscience is illusory. Social efficiency rather than moral excellence in the Christian sense becomes the ideal. The Christian virtues of restraint, submission, humility, obedience, respect for authority, and the theological virtues of Faith, Hope, and Charity lose their meaning. The idea is for men to devote themselves not to God but to improving society.

Perhaps the most representative statement of the atheistic position of intellectuals in contemporary America is in the *Humanist Manifesto* documents. These two manifestos constitute a kind of joint statement of the anti-religious position of a wide sampling of intellectuals with varying degrees of authority and from most of the intellectual disciplines. *Humanist Manifesto I* was published in 1933 under the aegis of John Dewey himself, and its main aim was to neutralize the influence of religion in the world. By contemporary standards, however, it treated religion rather gently. Its signers refer to themselves as "religious humanists," but the whole tenor of the manifesto is unfriendly to religion. The document was calculated to strip religion of all doctrine and to strip God of all power, including even the minimal function of creating the universe. "Religious humanists," it declares, "regard the universe as self-existing and not created." Furthermore, it insists that "the nature of the universe depicted by modern science makes unacceptable any supernatural or cosmic guarantees of human values," which is to say that among other things it repudiates the authority of the Scriptures.

The preface to *Humanist Manifesto II*, which was published in 1973, points out that *Humanist Manifesto I* was at the time a radical document in its rejection of Revelation and its commitment to reason-and-science, though actually the 19th century was full of intellectuals who would have subscribed to a far more anti-religious manifesto than it was. In the interests of greater honesty, *Humanist Manifesto II* dropped the epithet "religious" and instead used the term "humanist" without modification. Accordingly, the anti-religious spirit of the document is more nearly naked. "Humanists," the preface declares, "still believe that traditional theism, especially faith in a prayer-hearing God, assumed to love and care for persons, to hear and understand their prayers, and to be able to do something about them, is an unproved and outmoded faith."

The body of the document makes even clearer its

atheistic orientation: "We find insufficient evidence," it states, "for belief in the existence of the supernatural; it is either meaningless or irrelevant to the survival and fulfillment of the human race," and indeed it chastises any humanists who might want to "up-date" religion rather than to destroy it. Given such a premise, it of course comes down hard on any concept of personal immortality. "There is no credible evidence that life survives the death of the body," it declares, and "Promises of immortal salvation or fear of damnation are both illusory and harmful." These conclusions are based squarely upon the insistence that reason and particularly the senses are the only way to truth, and that therefore what cannot be perceived by the senses cannot be true. "Reason and intelligence," it insists, "are the most effective instruments that humankind possesses," and "the controlled use of scientific methods . . . must be extended further in the solution of human problems."

Humanist Manifesto II is in fact a highly optimistic document, and was intended partly as an antidote to those who view the world with despair. Its aim is high, nothing less in fact than the creation of a world in which "peace, prosperity, freedom, and happiness are widely shared." But so desirable a state, it insists, can be achieved only with the eradication of religion. It envisions a happy world of naturally good unbelievers who stake all on the authority of reason and science.

Despite the acknowledgement in *Humanist Manifesto II* of the limitations of reason and science, there is no sense of the dangers or limitations of a world without God. There is nothing of the sense of tragedy or loss which Nietzsche and Dostoevsky experienced as they imagined a world without God, and certainly there is nothing of the acute awareness of the consequences of

Solidifying the Post-Christian Age

unbelief of contemporary atheist existentialists. On the contrary, the premise of *Humanist Manifesto II* is that its laudable goals can be achieved only if religion is abolished.

I do not wish to overemphasize the importance of these *Humanist Manifestoes*, for the little band who signed them do not exert much collective influence, nor do they all agree with all the declarations in them; and most certainly have no taste for organized activism. But the 114 original signers of *Humanist Manifesto II* represent a fairly wide range of intellectual specialties. The list runs heavily to scientists, social scientists, and philosophers, though it also includes, interestingly enough, ministers and rabbis, a couple of poets, and the president of the Illinois Gas Company. The names of 150 more intellectuals have since been added, and no doubt by now thousands of additional names could be mustered.

Thus far I have emphasized in this chapter the role of philosophers in solidifying the post-Christian age, for their influence has probably been paramount. But certain theologians too have enjoyed an unprecedented influence in dismantling the Christian religion. Twentieth-century theologians do not have a corner on attacking the fundamental doctrines of Christianity, for as we have seen, heresies appeared almost as soon as Christianity appeared, and in the 19th century some theologians, such as Feuerbach, Strauss, and Renan, and experiments in Biblical criticism threatened Christianity almost as much as any 19th-century philosopher. But their influence on subsequent theological thought was somehow more limited than that of certain radical theologians of the 20th century who have contributed to the death-of-God movement.

It is true that this movement would not have been so important if the philosophers had not created the intellectual atmosphere in which theological radicalism could thrive. Just as John the Baptist told the people to make way for the coming of God to visit the world, long strings of influential philosophers, of whom Nietzsche was only the most spectacular, were telling the people to prepare for the death of God. It was merely a matter of time before they were joined by a chorus of influential theologians.

Perhaps the place to begin is not with the death-of-God theologians themselves, but rather with the 20th-century radical theologians who came out of Protestant Germany, in particular Rudolf Bultmann, Paul Tillich, and Dietrich Bonhoeffer. It may not seem fair to think of any of these theologians as the chief forerunners of the death-of-God movement, for they had the reputation and indeed the intention of saving Christianity in the 20th century, not of destroying it. But in the end, their thinking struck sharply and deeply at the very doctrines of traditional Christianity, and their influence has been so powerful that they have become major figures in intellectual history in the 20th century.

Rudolf Bultmann was born in 1884 in Oldenburg, Germany, and he was Professor of New Testament Studies at Marburg until 1951. He was in fact the most radical of the New Testament critics, and in the end virtually repudiated the Bible as a source of knowledge about God. At the core of much of his thought is his distinction between two kinds of experience, empirical and existential. Empirical experience deals with objects and events as they occur in the world, and they can be ordered, examined, explained, and can be used in the manipulation of the world. Existential experience, on the other hand, deals with the experience of being and asks such questions as "What is it like for me to be me?" and, "What does it mean for me to be me?" Bultmann insists that the existence of God cannot only not be demonstrated by reason; it cannot even be demonstrated by the Bible, which is itself mere empirical experience and describes merely empirical experience. Only from existential experience can anyone learn anything about God. In fact, with the help of atheistic existentialism, particularly in the teaching of Heidegger, Bultmann offered an existentialist interpretation of the New Testament which required a repudiation of any objective interpretation either of the historical Christ or of Christian doctrine. What is important, for example, is not the Cross or the Resurrection as objective historical events but as personal commitments in order to achieve an "authentic human existence," a term he borrowed from Heidegger. Christianity is not a matter of tradition, sacraments, ceremonies, historical events, or miracles, Bultmann insisted, but a matter of motivation and decision and interior encounter. Authentic existence, as Bultmann understand it, requires a commitment of faith in God, but without the support of the objective authority of the Bible, which he maintained can in fact tell us nothing about God. For Bultmann what is important is not the objective fact of whether Christ was or was not God, but rather the Christian message—but only the unique effect of the Christian message on each individual as an affirmation of his being, not as the basis of a doctrine of a Church or a universal moral law.

In effect, what Bultmann does in such works as *Kerygma and Myth* and *The New Testament and Mythology* is to attempt to undermine the authority of the fundamental doctrines and institutions and practices of Christianity and substitute for them a Christianity whose only function is to contribute to every individual's sense of "authentic existence" in this world.

Theology had a way to go beyond Bultmann's, before it achieved a truly atheistic status, for Bultmann did not propose that all the myths of Christianity be discarded, only those which the scientific mind found intolerable or which contributed nothing to (or possibly even prevented) the achievement of an "authentic existence." Indeed, he regarded himself as a theological conservative compared to the liberal theologians of the 19th century. But on balance, Bultmann's thought, its orginality, and its radical flavor have done much to undermine traditional Christian teaching and it has had a profound influence not only upon Protestant thought, but upon Catholic and Jewish thought as well and appears to have led more or less directly to the death-of-God theology of recent years.

An even more influential 20th-century theologian, perhaps even the most influential theologian, was Paul Tillich, who declared himself to be Bultmann's disciple. Tillich has reached a far larger audience than Bultmann and in many ways has superseded him in his influence. Tillich too was born in Germany, in 1886, the son of a Lutheran pastor. He was ordained into the Evangelical Lutheran Church in 1912. With the rise of the Hitler regime he moved to America, where he became Professor of Systematic Theology at Union Theological Seminary. He later taught at Harvard and the University of Chicago until his death in 1956. His early works, *The Religious Situation* and *The Interpretation of History*, were written in German and had to be translated for the English-speaking world. His later works, such as *The Courage to Be*, *The Dynamics of Faith*, and his most important work, *Systematic Theology*, were written in English and had to be translated for the German-speaking world.

Tillich harnessed his vast learning in the cause of Christianity with the aim of making it acceptable to the modern world, just as Bultmann tried to do. He too concluded that he had to repudiate most of the doctrines that historically had been keeping Christianity alive. It was not Tillich's intention to abandon the major doctrines of Christianity, but rather to deepen their meaning by interpreting them symbolically. This stance led him to deny utterly any literal interpretation of the Bible, and in fact he became so preoccupied with symbol and myth in the Bible that he came increasingly to ignore its historical significance. But the radical nature of Tillich's thought is perhaps best suggested by his famous concept of "absolute faith and the courage to be."

Tillich's concept of "the courage to be" provides the existential basis for his theology, and by it he means that the self-affirmation of God makes possible the self-affirmation of individual being—as opposed to non-being—which is an act of courage, and which gives the best evidence, indeed the only evidence, of the existence of God. By "absolute faith," Tillich means faith in "God above God." It does not mean faith in any visible authority, like the Church, or the Bible as the revealed word of God. It means, rather, that "absolute faith" has no content whatsoever. In fact, Tillich denied the existence of God as a Person. God is indeed personal, but He is not a Person.

Tillich was convinced that the authority of science had become too potent in the 20th century to permit any longer a belief in a traditional interpretation of the divine nature of the historical Christ. As a result, he interpreted such fundamental Christian doctrines as the Incarnation, the Atonement, and Trinity as merely symbols. Any literal interpretation of these doctrines was, he insisted, absurd; the same held true for such fundamental Christian concepts as sin and grace and prayer, which also must be reduced to symbols. Like Tolstoy, the more Christian doctrines he jettisoned, the more messianic he became in the name of Christianity, for he thought of himself above all as a teacher and a preacher, whose role it was to accommodate the teachings of the Bible to the "problems of our day." He wanted man to increase his consciousness of God and to become a "new being," a phenomenon best achievable through an understanding of the symbolic meaning of the historical Jesus. God, he insisted, has never interposed Himself in any way in man's world and never will.

Tillich is so complex a thinker that the radical character of his theology is not always recognized, although the atheistic implications of his thinking have not gone altogether unnoticed. In any case, Tillich has gone farther perhaps than any other theologian in his repudiation of Christian doctrine, while at the same time supposing that he was promoting, indeed preserving, Christianity.

Both Bultmann and Tillich were army chaplains in World War I, and both desperately wanted to make Christianity intelligible to a suffering and disillusioned world. But they felt that in order to do so they had to adjust the teaching of Christianity to a scientific world, and that meant giving up those doctrines which would not pass the scientific test, that is to say, most of them. In fact it may be possible to accept Bultmann's position and Tillich's as well, without believing in any God at all. And yet their passionate belief in less and less made them seem all the more Christian, in comparison to more orthodox theologians who believed much less passionately in far more. It certainly made them more influential.

Dietrich Bonhoeffer was another major thinker who came out of the tradition of liberal European Protestantism and who was much concerned to make Christianity meaningful to the modern world. Bonhoeffer's active resistance to the Nazi regime and his heroic death (he was hanged in one of Hitler's concentration camps) has called special attention to his writings, particularly to his *Letters and Papers from Prison*. Of almost equal fascination are his involvement in an ecumenical movement and his leadership in a clandestine seminary in Germany. Sometimes his rather spectacular life and death seem to obscure that fact of his brilliance and wide learning.

Bonhoeffer may seem to have been a less radical theologian than either Tillich or Bultmann, but ultimately he may have been even more so. It is true that Bonhoeffer was inspired by Karl Barth, who represented an almost reactionary theological position, whereas Bultmann owed most to Barth's theological opposite, Martin Heidegger. Yet Bonhoeffer, Tillich, and Bultmann were ultimately lined up on the same side. Whereas Barth emphasized the supernatural and the absolute unsymbolic interpretation of the Bible, the others all aimed at accommodating and adjusting the Bible to modern man. Barth wanted modern man to adjust himself to the Bible. As we have seen, Bultmann and Tillich made massive readjustments, and in his way Bonhoeffer did too. He too de-emphasized the authority of the church and downplayed the role of doctrine and ritual. He insisted that God had never intervened in man's world, and he repudiated any literal interpretation of the Bible. Bonhoeffer's chief complaint about Bultmann's efforts to demythologize the New Testament is that he did not go far enough. "It is not only the mythological conceptions, such as the miracles, the ascension and the like . . . that are problematic," he declares, "but the 'religious' conceptions themselves. You cannot, as Bultmann imagines, separate God and miracles, but you do have to be able to interpret and proclaim both of them in a 'non-religious' sense."

On the doctrine of immortality, which is central to traditional Christianity, he is no less provocative: "Is it not true to say," he asks, "that individualistic concern for personal salvation has almost completely left us all? Are we not really under the impression that there are more important things than-bothering about such a matter? (Perhaps not more important than the matter itself, but more than bothering about it.) I know it sounds pretty monstrous to say that. But is it not, at bottom, even Biblical? Is there any concern in the Old Testament about saving one's soul at all? . . . It is not the next world that we are concerned about but this world as created and preserved and set, subject to laws and atoned for and made new. What is above the world is, in the Gospel, intended to exist for *this* world."

There are at times strong suggestions in the *Letters* that man does not need God at all, as for example in this observation:

> Man has learned to cope with all questions of importance without recourse to God as a working hypothesis. In questions concerning science, art and even ethics, this has become an understood thing which one scarcely dares to tilt at any more. But for the last hundred years or so it has been increasingly true of religious questions also: It is becoming evident that everything gets along without 'God' and just as well as before.

It is not possible to put together a system of theology from the informal nature of Bonhoeffer's *Letters*, but it may be that he comes closer to sentiments of downright atheism than either Bultmann or Tillich. "There is no longer any need for God as a working hypothesis," he writes in one letter, "whether in morals, politics, or science. Nor is there any need for such a God in religion or philosophy (Feuerbach). In the name of intellectual honesty, those working hypotheses should be dropped or dispensed with as far as possible."

Ultimately it may be that Bonhoeffer's contribution to the preservation of Christianity in the modern world will come not through his works but through his life.

The death-of-God theologians are commonly thought of as radical, but as we have seen, Bultmann, Tillich, and Bonhoeffer were themselves radical theologians, in that all the while they were writing about Christ, God, and faith they were hacking away at the very roots of Christianity, a fact which gives them a certain right to the epithet "radical." If, then, they were themselves radical theologians, what are the death-of-God theologians? Essentially they were anti-theists, anti-theists in much the same sense in which I have been using the term to designate the French Enlighteners and a whole host of intellectuals throughout the 19th and 20th centuries; i.e., they regarded Christianity as a major barrier to man's progress and well-being, they welcomed atheism and indeed proclaimed it as a measure of man's intellectual progress, and they were suspicious of all religious institutions, rituals, and dogmas. They were not philosophers, like Hobbes, Nietzsche, and Dewey; they were theologians like St. Thomas Aquinas, Luther, and Newman, except that they repudiated virtually every fundamental doctrine Christianity has ever professed. If their hostility toward institutional Christianity did not rival that of Nietzsche or Freud or Lenin, they rejoiced quite as much at the prospect of a dead God, and at man living very well, if not better, without Him. But it is the fact that they attacked religion from the inside as theologians rather than from the outside as philosophers, that gave them their special significance, and vastly increased their influence.

The hardest-core death-of-God theologians were both Americans, William Hamilton and Thomas J. J. Altizer, who represented the *ne plus ultra* of the movement; but closely akin to them were the Anglican bishop and theologian John A. T. Robinson, author of *Honest to God*, and Harvey Cox, author of *The Secular City*. Other seminal thinkers in the movement included Paul M. Van Buren, whose book *The Secular Meaning of the Gospel* provides an excellent demonstration of how analytical or linguistic philosophy in the tradition of Wittgenstein can destroy the authority of the Scriptures. Gabriel Vahanian, too, a French Protestant theologian, who migrated to America, also played a significant role in the movement, especially with his books *The Death of God* and *Wait Without Idols*. Vahanian started out as a disciple of Karl Barth, but many disciples of Karl Barth react so strongly to his Biblical Christianity and orthodox fideism that they end up in the death-of-God camp, and Vahanian was one of them. His intense negativism led him beyond the radicalism of the radical theologians. He began where Bonhoeffer left off, i.e., with the "religionless Christianity" of Bonhoeffer's *Letters*, by insisting that we must not only live with the cultural fact that God is dead but we should rejoice in it.

But Robinson, Hamilton, and Altizer were the most influential theologians to the left of the radical theologians. Robinson's book *Honest to God* (which, in effect, means "Honest, there is no God") appeared in 1963

Solidifying the Post-Christian Age   167

and put him at the head of the movement in the sense that before his book appeared the movement had not been formed. The book went so far beyond the thinking of Tillich and Bonhoeffer that it caused something of a theological storm. It was, in its way, an eclectic book inasmuch as it embraced the demythologizing of Christianity which Bultmann wanted, the stripping of the supernatural from Christianity which Tillich wanted, and the deleting of the "religiousness" of Christianity which Bonhoeffer wanted. Robinson was also profoundly influenced by the atheistic evolutionism of Julian Huxley.

In *Honest to God*, Robinson compares the revolution in theology with the Copernican revolution, suggesting that modern man can no more believe in God than he can in the Ptolemaic theory of the universe. The supernatural interpretation of the Christian mysteries and the idea of a personal God, he held, are preposterous. His book in effect would appear to announce the end of theism, and with it the death of theology.

In some ways the atheism of Robinson's Christianity is more explicit in his later book *The New Reformation*, in which he explains how well modern man can get along without God. God is, first of all, he insists, "intellectually superfluous," because belief in God has in fact held up scientific progress, which is the kind of progress upon which all truth must now be built. Second, God is "emotionally unnecessary," inasmuch as men now believe in themselves and in others and that not only do men not need God in their emotional development, but He is no real help in facing the real difficulties of life in any case. Third, God is "morally intolerable," because belief in God is a major cause of suffering and tragedy. It is not so much that these arguments are new, for they have in fact been advanced over and over again from the time of the Enlighteners, and before, but Bishop Robinson illustrated how he, as a theologian, had also been enlightened, not only by the light of reason, but by the light of science. Ultimately all that Bishop Robinson could recommend was a personal faith; it could be a faith in anyone or anything, though preferably not in the doctrines of Christianity. An atheist with a perfect faith in science, it turns out, may in fact be the most religious of all men.

But the theologians most closely connected with the death-of-God movement are William Hamilton, Professor of Theology at Colgate Rochester Divinity School, and Thomas J. J. Altizer, Professor of Religion at Emory University. The concept of the death-of-God is as old as the Enlightenment. The term itself is associated with Nietzsche, but the popularization or special use of it is attributable to Hamilton and Altizer, even more than to Van Buren, whose book bears the title *The Death of God*. What is meant or could be meant by the phrase "death of God" has been the subject of much speculation, but what Hamilton and Altizer appear to mean by it is that God has died because men no longer find Him believable or useful; hence it must be that God never really existed except in men's imaginations. He must, therefore, never have really existed, but we are only now discovering the fact, and thanks to science and reason and to such thinkers as Bultmann, Tillich, and Bonhoeffer—and themselves—we can all breathe a sigh of relief. Altizer and Hamilton were much taken with the religious zeal with which their intellectual predecessors disbelieved, and, not to be outdone, with comparable zeal they disbelieved in even more.

If it is sometimes difficult to pin down what these fore-runners of the death-of-God theologians did not believe in, it is less of a problem with Hamilton and Altizer. "Never before," wrote Altizer, "has faith been called upon to negate all *religious* meaning." "Consequently the theologian must exist outside the church; he can neither proclaim the Word, celebrate the Sacraments, nor rejoice in the presence of the Holy Spirit." Hamilton is even less equivocal: "I am denying that religion is necessary," he declares. "I do not see how preaching, worship, prayer, ordination, and the Sacraments can be taken seriously by the radical theologian." And Hamilton is a radical theologian if there ever was one.

How much farther can a theologian go as a disbeliever? It may be that Altizer and Hamilton have reached the limit. And it is characteristic that they should be Americans, for American intellectuals appear, for a number of reasons, to be in the front ranks of comfortable unbelievers. Rarely does one catch the most influential American intellectuals in any serious condition of anguish or agony at the thought of the implications of the non-existence of God. American intellectual history has produced no believers like Kierkegaard or Dosttoevsky, who have communicated so powerfully an understanding of the consequences of unbelief, nor indeed any unbelievers like Nietzsche or Camus, who have plumbed the depths of what it means to give up God. In the intellectual history of the Western world, American intellectuals are among the most unthoughtful of thinkers.

The death-of-God movement represented the ultimate clash between the contradictions concerning what philosophy and science seem to be telling men and what their religion has been telling them. The death-of-God movement represents the total triumph of the faculties of man's reason and his senses as the ultimate authority in the search for truth, and hence the ultimate defeat of the authority of Revelation in the form of Scripture. Whereas in earlier centuries the great enemies of Christianity were philosophers and scientists, now they have been joined by the theologians. And if theologians no longer defend Christianity, then who will—at least who will who can match the authority of the philosophers, scientists, and theologians?

CHAPTER VIII

CHRISTIAN INTELLECTUALS IN A POST-CHRISTIAN AGE

The evidence that the most influential thinkers of the 20th century have taken command and solidified the post-Christian age appears to be overwhelming, as the previous chapter of this study has suggested. Christianity seems not only thoroughly devastated by three centuries of anti-Christian thought outside the Church, but more recently undermined by subtle yet lethal intellectual forces within the Church. The traditional doctrines of Christianity seem to find no purchase on the slippery, stony philosophical mind-set of most intellectuals, major or minor, of the contemporary world.

And yet the dominant thinkers of the present age have not gone wholly unchallenged in their conclusion that civilization has outgrown Christianity, and that indeed religion is a major hindrance to advancement and progress. The 20th century has also produced Christian intellectuals, and influential ones too. They have demonstrated both courage and faith in attempting to counteract the relentless erosion of the fundamental doctrines of Christianity, even by theologians, and to challenge the philosophers' axiom that reason and science, not the Bible and Christianity, are the way to truth. In the 19th century, powerful intellectuals like

Kierkegaard, Newman, and Dostoevsky dared take on the entire intellectual establishment of their times with a zeal, and sometimes even a relish, and, more important, with a skill and a genius which even today gives thoughtful anti-Christian thinkers pause. Has the 20th century produced comparable defenders of the Christian faith? Perhaps not, but there are major Christian intellectuals in the 20th century who have challenged the intellectual establishment in its increasingly comfortable, even smug, acceptance of the idea that Christ was not God, that the Bible is not God's Revelation, and indeed, that God does not exist. How large a role these Christians will play in the intellectual history of the 20th century when it is told a hundred or two hundred years hence is by no means certain. It may well be a very minor role. But it is well to remind ourselves that intellectuals of genius in the 20th century have, with considerable success, stated the case for Christianity in a post-Christian age.

As we have seen, such intellectuals as Bultmann, Bonhoeffer, and Tillich spent their energies and genius trying to make Christianity acceptable to the modern world, but in the process seem to have given away so much of it that, in the end, they led more or less directly to the death-of-God theology. This chapter is concerned with some of the seminal 20th-century thinkers who also strove to make Christianity understood—received—by the modern world, but who at the same time refused to yield up its most crucial doctrines, those doctrines which have ever been its hallmark and its heart.

Among these were two Swiss intellectuals, Karl Barth and Emil Brunner. Their thinking ran squarely against not only the dominant scientific rationalism of 20th-century European philosophy, but also against the firmly-entrenched liberalism of Protestant theology. Karl

Barth is universally regarded as one of the most important Protestant theologians of the 20th century, sometimes even with the suggestion that he is another Luther or another Calvin. And indeed, like Luther and Calvin, he widened the gap between God and man which liberal theology had almost succeeded in closing, and he did so chiefly by restoring the doctrine of Original Sin to Protestant theology. He also attempted to put science and philosophy in their places by demonstrating that neither method of arriving at truth can attain the most important truths. Reason, he reminded his fellow intellectuals in a book significantly titled *The Word of God and the Word of Man* "sees the small and the larger, but not the large. It sees the preliminary but not the final, the derived but not the original, the complex but not the simple. It sees what is human but not what is divine." And if reason tells us so little, then the senses, the only method admissible to science, tell us even less.

The philosophers and scientists, he insisted, must yield to the theologians in the quest for ultimate truth. But he found that the theologians were collapsing in the presence of the authority of reason-and-science; the great God-given truths were yielding to the minor man-perceived truths. But Barth stuck to his guns. He proposed to re-form perception. He was thus a genuine reformer, not so much a moral reformer as an epistemological reformer, and a theological reformer. By restoring the doctrine of Original Sin, which so many theologians had abandoned, he restored the doctrines of the Incarnation, the Atonement, and the Resurrection, as well as many other Christian doctrines which have no meaning except in the context of the doctrine of Original Sin. By insisting upon the proper distance between man and God he hoped also to restore some intellectual humility among the intellectuals, for among intellectuals intellectual pride is something of an occupational disease. The most important fact about God, Barth insisted, is that He is God, He is "the Wholly Other." God is not so much a "Becoming" as Hegel and his followers believed, or a "Has Been" as even some theologians had come to believe; He is an "Always Has Been," not an immanent God, as modern theologians think, but a transcendent God as traditional theologians have always thought. He is not "Being," as the existentialists tried to make Him, sometimes in order to get rid of Him, but He is "a Being," who will always be above and beyond the merely human. In fact, Barth insisted that the sense of alienation and meaninglessness which afflicts the 20th century came in part because intellectuals required God to accommodate Himself endlessly to Man. What God thinks about man, he insisted, is more important than what man thinks about God. "Let God be God," he said, just as Luther had said more than three centuries before. And God is the God who was in Christ and is in Christ, and He speaks to man through Christ and through the Bible. The Bible is in fact the best source for learning a knowledge of God. To look elsewhere is to assume that we know better than God who He is. The Bible is neither philosophy nor poetry nor history; it is above all Divine Revelation, God speaking to man. "It is not the right human thoughts about God which form the content of the Bible, but the right divine thoughts about men." And he goes on:

> The Bible tells us not how we should talk with God but what He says to us; not how we find the way to Him, but how He has sought and found the way to us; not the right relation in which we must place ourselves to Him, but the Covenant which He has made with all who are Abraham's spiritual children and which he has sealed once and for all in Jesus

Christ. It is this which is within the Bible. The Word of God is within the Bible.

In arriving at these conclusions he was not unaware of the opposite direction in which philosophy and theology were taking mankind. On the contrary, he started out on his intellectual odyssey in the company of the chief representatives of Protestant liberalism. He even studied in Berlin under Adolph von Harnack, the ultimate in fashionable liberal theology, and for a time he fell under the spell of religious socialism, as Tillich did, and he established himself as a brilliant and sophisticated young liberal.

But in time, his thinking took him beyond theirs. Whereas they seemed always on the defensive in attempting to justify Christianity and above all to compromise it in a post-Christian world dominated by scientific rationalism, Barth began insisting upon the limitations of scientific rationalism in arriving at truth, and proposed what had been rejected, if not wholly forgotten—namely the Bible as the key to the truth of God and the happiness of man.

He saw the leading Protestant theologians as remaking Christianity in man's own image. He saw that they thought that the Reformation did not go far enough, that Christians must be freed not only from the tyranny of the Roman Pope, but also from the Bible. He observed that they had concluded that the Old Testament was for Jews, not Christians, and that the validity of the Gospels was doubtful and that Christ may not even have existed. He observed further that having denied that men suffered from the Fall, they supposed they were leading men up a rosy path to a moral Utopia, but were actually leading them into the maelstrom of Absolute Relativism and hence to moral chaos.

Barth himself in his early years engaged to some degree in this kind of thinking, but a number of influences, not all easily identifiable, led him to blow the whistle on the progress of liberal theology. The conservative eye of his father, the somewhat conservative thinking of his brother Heinrich, the readiness of many liberal intellectuals, including many of his former theological teachers, to embrace the Kaiser and his war policy, the influence of Kierkegaard, the discovery of Dostoevsky's insights into the plight of man as sinner, his close study of St. Paul's *Epistle to the Romans*, and doubtless many other factors caused him to abandon the liberal camp and to launch a one-man neo-Reformation. He spent some of his best rhetorical efforts attacking liberal Protestant theology from the time of its founder, Schleiermacher up to his own time. The keenness of his sense of the danger they presented to Christianity is suggested by the following passage:

> If I today became convinced that the interpretation of the Reformation on the line taken by Schleiermacher—Ritschl—Troeltsch (or even Seeberg or Holl) was correct; that Luther and Calvin really intended such an outcome of their labors: I could not indeed become a Catholic tomorrow, but I should have to withdraw from the evangelical Church. And if I were forced to make a choice between the two evils, I should, in fact, prefer the Catholic.

Barth's writings in defense of neo-Orthodox Protestantism are massive and range from his early commentary on St. Paul's Epistle to the Romans to his 13-volume, 9,000-page *Dogmatic Theology* which may be the most comprehensive interpretation of the Christian faith in modern theology.

Emil Brunner was another of the few major intellectuals to become seriously alarmed at the direction which the mainstream of religious thought was taking in the 20th century, a mainstream which carried liberal Protestant theology along on the surface and downright atheism beneath. Brunner, too, was nurtured in the same liberal tradition as Barth, having done his theological studies under its major professors at Zurich and Berlin. He even lectured at the Union Theological Seminary in New York at a time when religious liberalism there was at its zenith. He became involved in the work of the World Council of Churches and the Moral Re-armament Movement, and generally accepted the emphasis which liberal theologians placed on the social and ethical aspects of the Bible. He accepted, too, their emphasis upon a rationalized theology which was enhanced by his own interest in philosophy. He even wrote a learned and sympathetic study of the thought of Edmund Husserl, the founder of phenomenology, with its insistence upon the scientizing of philosophy.

But after World War I, he, like Barth, turned on his liberal mentors and colleagues and began to attack the whole liberal tradition in Protestant theology. The conviction grew on him that if Protestantism did not undergo a major reformation, it was in danger of collapse. "The Protestant theology of our day," he declared in *The Theology of Crisis*, "is in a stage of rapid dissolution . . . The substance of Christian theology, the content of Christian faith, is in a state of complete decomposition. Christianity is either faith in the revelation of God in Jesus Christ or it is nothing." Like Barth, he proceeded to launch an attack on the whole liberal school, from Schleiermacher through Albrecht Ritschl and Adolph von Harnack, as well as its principal representatives in England and America. He particularly attacked Schleiermacher's belief that all men are naturally religious and that therefore Christianity will come naturally. Brunner insisted that Christian Revelation is distinctive and cannot be arrived at from natural theology or private experience. He concluded that the God of philosophy cannot be the God of Christianity, and that the role of philosophy is above all to demonstrate that human reason is too limited to comprehend God's Revelation through the Scriptures.

Yet Brunner did not repudiate philosophy as a means to truth as Barth did, and in fact he admitted that Biblical criticism in the liberal tradition had scored some points in calling attention to discrepancies in the Bible. The authority of science, he felt, would never permit a return to orthodoxy. Such concessions brought him into conflict with Barth, and a heated controversy between them and their followers ensued. Barth replied to Brunner in a work called *NO! An Angry Answer to Emil Brunner*, in which he reminded Brunner that man was totally corrupted by the Fall and that his natural powers could never advance him so much as an inch toward God.

But the point here is that Brunner would not compromise the fundamental doctrines of Christianity as liberal Protestantism had done, and in attempting to find a middle way between liberalism and orthodoxy he came to be regarded as a champion of "neo-orthodoxy." He was sufficiently orthodox to support the doctrine of the Trinity and hence the Incarnation, so that liberals cannot claim him as theirs, however hard they sometimes try. He stated his case for neo-orthodoxy, not only in his three-volume *Dogmatics*, but in a host of other scholarly books and articles, in which he demonstrated how a brilliant intellectual need not succumb to the tyranny of reason-and-science, which had led to atheism among philosophers and other intellectuals who were not theologians, and to liberalism among those who were. For good measure, he lectured and travelled throughout the world and left in his wake a string of sermons, lectures, and semi-popular books not to the advantage of either atheistic intellectuals or liberal Protestants.

Still another powerful thinker who swam against the swift intellectual currents of the 20th century was Jacques Maritain, who, like Barth and Brunner, was brought up on liberal Protestantism, but who in time became a Catholic. Maritain was as passionate a searcher after truth as any intellectual in the 20th century, and perhaps as powerful a thinker. He was, in addition, a man of universal learning and made his mark in religion, history, politics, and the arts. He was, above all, however, a philosopher, and the author of some 50 books and countless articles on virtually every aspect of philosophy and cultural life. His writings indicate that he achieved a highly developed social, moral, and political philosophy, as well as a philosophy of art and of religion. He is the complete intellectual.

He was born in Paris in 1882 and nourished, not on Catholicism, but on liberal Protestantism, like Barth and Brunner. Like them too, he received massive exposure to the dominant scientific rationalism of his professors, so that for a time he may hardly have had a spiritual thought in his head. At the Sorbonne he met Raissa Oumansoff, a brilliant Russian Jewish student, who was also passionately searching for the truth, and who became his wife. She wrote of herself that, even at age 14,

> Before all else, I had to make sure of the essential thing: the possession of truth about God, about myself, and about the world. It was, I knew, the necessary foundation of my life; I could not, without letting the ground be washed away from under me, give up the pursuit of its discovery.

These words might as easily have been written by Maritain himself, and so together they set out to find the truth within the confines of the Sorbonne. They inhaled the absolute relativism, the intellectual skepticism, and the moral nihilism of the prevailing philosophical atmosphere, but soon concluded that the truth was not to be found where most of the faculty said it was to be found, namely in science. They refused to yield to the tyranny of the senses. They then attended the lectures of Henri Bergson, who taught at the College de France across the street from the Sorbonne, for Bergson was a bit of a buffer against the hard-core scientism which informed the thinking of most intellectuals. In time, however, they concluded, as Maritain said, that Bergson was "too flimsy a refuge" against the intellectual nihilism which they were encountering at every turn.

They were at this time ripe for the influence of Leon Bloy, the Catholic mystic whose denunciation of materialism and wealth gave him something of the air of a 20th-century St. Francis. They read his novel *The Woman Who Was Poor*, which led Raissa to exclaim that "for the first time we found ourselves before the reality of Christianity." After some serious spiritual struggles, they were baptised into the Catholic faith, and all their thinking and writing henceforth was done within the framework of their Catholicism. After the death of Raissa, who was at once his inspiration and collaborator, Maritain abandoned Princeton University, where he taught for a time, to spend the remainder of his years in Toulouse with the Little Brothers of Jesus.

But during all the years of his writing and thinking Maritain did not take on the members of the intellectual establishment by throwing Christian mysticism at them. What he threw at them was a whole epistemology which insisted that science and the senses are only one way of arriving at truth, and an inferior kind of truth at that. Unlike Barth, however, he did not dismiss the scientific method or indeed the rational method, i.e., the method of philosophy. Rather he enlisted philosophy and science in arriving at a higher and more crucial kind of truth, the truth of God and His relation to men. In these endeavors he sought out the thinking of Aristotle and Aquinas, and in fact became a latter-day Christian humanist. He thus introduced neo-Thomism to the 20th century. He insisted that Thomism is quite as viable today as it was in the Middle Ages and he proceeded to outline a monumental synthesis of science, philosophy, and theology, not unlike Aquinas himself in his *Summa Theologiae*. Even today, his work on the philosophy of history has not been very seriously challenged, even though it had no couterpart in Aquinas's thought. What in effect Maritain was saying is that Aquinas's great synthesis between philosophy and theology is capable of endless development and can assimilate an accumulation of all kinds of truths, including scientific and historical truths.

Thus, in a sense, Maritain did for Aquinas what Karl Barth did for Augustine, though Maritain leaned on Augustine too. In any case, what Barth, Brunner, and Maritain did was to stab the intellectual establishment in its tender epistemological underbelly and demonstrate that its representatives were seeking truth in a little corner of the universe of truth and were destined ultimately to mistake minor truths for major truths.

Gabriel Marcel, a countryman of Jacques Maritain, also deserves to be placed in the first rank of Christian intellectuals in the 20th century, and, like Maritain, he had his fingers in any number of intellectual pies. He produced not only a truly impressive quantity and quality of seminal philosophical writing; he was also a substantial dramatist, a professional drama and music critic, and a musician. Like Maritain, too, he did not begin his life as a Catholic but was brought up in a religiously skeptical household. As his religious sensibilities developed he was at first more inclined to Protestantism than to Catholicism. His education at the Sorbonne led him to Hegel and the idealist tradition in philosophy, but he rebelled against the strait jacket of philosophical systems, and adopted an increasingly existentialist stance, from which position his own original philosophical thought begins.

But he was not to go the atheistic route of Sartre and Camus. He confessed that he had "always been partial to religion even when he belonged to no determined confession," and after a series of spiritual peregrinations he entered the Catholic Church in 1929 at the age of 39, and proceeded to become one of the two or three greatest Christian existentialists of the 20th century. He became the philosopher of faith and hope, not the philosopher of futility and meaningless, which was the direction that existentialism was taking among most intellectuals. He found himself in the position of taking on not only atheistic existentialism, but also the now-dominant view in the intellectual world that science and only science can be trusted to solve man's problems and to arrive at the truest truths. His intellectual enemies were therefore the same as Barth's, Brunner's, and Maritain's.

Like most existentialists, he was highly skeptical of the claims that most intellectuals were making for science, but unlike most existentialists he was not anti-religious. Truth was to be found not in the I-It relationship, but in the I-Thou relationship, and the

"Thou" was God, as well as man. Where Sartre and Camus were calling for a commitment to anything but God, Marcel was calling for a commitment above all to God, and not some deistic God but the God of Christianity, who had revealed Himself to man through the Scriptures. Faith thus becomes the supreme virtue for Marcel and hope, the second. Faith in God can lead to absolute fidelity, an unconditional surrender of self. What is most important in life, he insisted, is not belief in something but in someone, and above all in Someone, the Absolute Thou, from whence all life and being take their substance and their meaning. On the subject of hope, Marcel observed in his *Homo Viator* that "I am inclined to believe that hope is for the soul what breathing is for the living organism," and he refused to accept Camus' assessment of the plight of the man in The *Myth of Sisphus*. Instead of arriving at Camus' conclusion that God could not have created a world so full of misery, Marcel writes that "Only in a world that really can suffer damage is there place for salvation."

These are not the conclusions of naive desperation. As Marcel's long list of philosophical works and plays will testify, he is one of the most thoughtful intellectuals that the 20th century has produced.

Another major representative of the Christian existentialist phenomenon was Miguel de Unamuno, who was the dominant intellectual of Spain in the early 20th century, and to some degree still is. He was born in Bilbao of Basque origin, educated in Madrid and spent most of his life as a professor and later as Rector of the University of Salamanca. He was perhaps the most universally read man of his time, being thoroughly at home in the major European languages and, in addition, a classical scholar. Having been profoundly influenced by the thinking of Kierkegaard, he was perhaps the most eloquent of this century's great Christian existentialists. As a result, he had much in common with Gabriel Marcel, both in his existential orientation and in his refusal to go the route of atheistic existentialism as Camus and Sartre were to do. Like Marcel he rejected the sense of meaninglessness, alienation, nihilism, and despair which became so characteristic of mainline existentialism. Also like Marcel, he developed a theology of faith and hope. Like Marcel too, and indeed like most existentialist thinkers, he elaborated no formal philosophical system, but rather expressed his ideas and feelings in imaginative literature, in plays and poetry and novels, his chosen vehicles for communicating his subjective and intuitive and, indeed mystical, experiences.

Like all the other Christian intellectuals of the first order he came to reject the intellectual currents of scientific materialism which dominated European thought in the early 20th century, even though he had been brought up in the positivistic tradition. But his discovery of Kierkegaard helped him to understand that the easy and comfortable solutions of the positivists and evolutionists did not even ask the right questions and, limited as they were by their exclusive commitment to the scientific method, they could never arrive at the answers. He even wrote a novel entitled *Love and Pedagogy* in which he demonstrated the failure of science in dealing with human problems by describing a man's attempt to educate his family scientifically and the tragic failure of the attempt. Many of his early works were foreshadowings of his masterpeice, *The Tragic Sense of Life*, in which he dealt most fully with the major philosophical problems which occupied, indeed, tortured him for much of his life. Among them were the fundamental problem of the meaning of existence, the universal yearning for immortality, the problems of guilt and anxiety and suffering which universally plague men, and the search for solace and faith and hope in a sorrowful world. He found it in religion, in Christianity, and more especially in the Catholicism of his own country. And yet this commitment to Christianity came hard, for even though his emotions pulled him toward the Church, his reason continued to pull him away from it. But it may well have been his reason that led him to Christianity, for he shared with Kierkegaard and Dostoevsky the most intense comprehension of the consequences of man in a world without God. He never ceased to be appalled at the naiveté of the dominant intellectual view that happiness is to be found, if at all, through evolutionary progress, with the necessary help of science. Religion, not science, is man's only hope, for only in religion can the answers to the really important questions be found. And "the road that leads us to the living God, the God of the heart, and that leads us back to Him when we have left Him for the lifeless God of logic," he wrote in *The Tragic Sense of Life*, "is the road of faith, not of rational or mathematical conviction." His own peculiar formula for coming to know God is first of all "Wishing that God may exist, and acting and feeling as if He did exist. And desiring God's existence and acting comformably with his desire, is the means whereby we create God—that is, whereby God creates Himself in us, manifests Himself to us, opens and reveals Himself to us." From thence, faith in the truths of Revelation in the Bible will then become authoritative and open the way for belief in all those fundamental doctrines of Christianity which take their authority from the Bible.

Even though he himself never came to accept all the doctrines of his native religion, he died in the certainty that his faith in Christianity and hence his understanding of man was far closer to the truth than was that of his atheistic brethren in France, Germany, England, and America, who were determining to a far greater degree the direction which philosophical thought was to take. He, too, confronted the Void, and his passionate exhortation, "If it is indeed nothingness that awaits us after death, let us so live that it will be an *injustice!*" still rings in our ears.

Christian existentialists have been among the most compelling defenders of Christianity against its most powerful 20th-century detractors, especially against the scientific materialists, because they perceived, probably better than the materialists, that the great truths of life and the meaning of life transcend scientific fact. They also perceived that religion, specifically Christianity, is the best way to avoid the conclusions of the atheist existentialists that life is at bottom meaningless and that, as Camus concluded in *The Myth of Sisyphus*, there is no wholly justifiable reason for living.

Another Christian existentialist, the seminal Russian thinker Nikolai Berdyaev, joined Unamuno and Gabriel Marcel in reaffirming that life is not meaningless and that there are wholly justifiable reasons for living, provided that the reasons are sought in religion, which to Berdayaev meant Christianity. Berdayaev started his spiritual odyssey from ground zero. He was brought up as a Marxist and a passionate one at that. Even though he had problems from the beginning with the materialism of Marxism, he nonetheless belonged to the extreme left wing of Marxist revolutionaries and he showed a messianic dedication to their cause. His political collaborators were Lunacharsky, Bogdanov, and Plekhanov, who were to be ranked among the foremost leaders of the Bolshevik Revolution in 1917. He even suffered three years exile under Czar Nicholas for his beliefs and after the revolution was rewarded with a professorship in philosophy at the University of Moscow. But when it became evident that his views were moving away from Marxism, he was exiled again and helped set up an Academy of Religion and Philosophy in Berlin, and then moved it to Paris in 1924.

Berdyaev's independence of mind and his gift for philosophical speculation caused him to pass from Marxism to idealism and ultimately to Christianity. His reading of Kant and Hegel led him to idealism, but his early concern with the problem of existence, which he came to regard as the central philosophical problem, seemed from the beginning to have a religious connotation for him and perhaps does much to explain why he went on to read the works of religious philosophers. He therefore proceeded to read the works of Schelling and F. X. von Baader, through whom he discovered Jacob Boehme, the 16th-century German mystic, as well as the major intellectuals of his own country such as the slavophiles, including Khomiakov, Kireyersky, Solovyev, and Vassily Rozanov. He was also influenced by the works of Tolstoy and especially of Dostoevsky. His book on Dostoevsky's religious thought is in fact better than any that has yet appeared.

During the course of his life, Berdyaev wrote 27 books and countless articles reaffirming the Christian position against the prevailing intellectual forces in Europe. Most of his writings are polemical and controversial, for like Kierkegaard and Dostoevsky, he recognized that he was taking on virtually the entire intellectual establishment in Europe. He avoided the compromising of Christian doctrine which the liberal Christian thinkers were engaged in, and he was forever opposing the scientific materialism which dominated the thinking not only of Marxism, but which was pandemic in Western Europe and America.

Like so many existentialist thinkers, Berdyaev not only avoided systematic philosophy; he never distinguished very clearly between his metaphysics and his religious and social thinking, and there is very little emphasis in his works on Biblical Christianity. But in his tragic sense of life, which he shared with all the great Christian existentialists, in his concern over the problem of freedom, the meaning of human existence, and in his wide-ranging writings on ethics, he found the best answer in Christianity.

But Berdyaev's Christianity was Eastern, not Western. It was not the Protestant neo-Reformation Christianity of Karl Barth or the neo-Thomist Catholicism of Maritain; it was the Christianity of Russian Orthodoxy, which strongly emphasizes the mystical, and the suprarational, and which is so largely alien to Western thought. In fact, much of what appears to be Western existentialism in Berdyaev's thought may be Eastern mysticism, and he is therefore easily misread by Western intellectuals. Western thinkers can hardly understand what Berdyaev means when he says that philosophy is "illumination," or what his fellow Orthodox thinker Solovyev means when he calls it "a mystical and intuitive doctrine of wisdom."

In his book *Symbolism, Myth and Dogma*, Berdyaev dissassociated himself from the Christianity of the rationalistic West, and in fact insisted that the purely rational thought of philosophy and systematic theology can provide no genuine knowledge of God. He insisted that there can be no philosophy without faith, and specifically without the Christian faith; but it is not faith in authority, which is so important to Western Catholicism, but faith won independently of an external authority, faith, as he says in *Freedom and the Spirit*, "through an experience of the inner life of a most painful character, through freedom."

And yet Orthodox Christianity has more in common with traditional Western Christianity than it has differences. Their Christ is the same, their New Testament is the same, and their fundamental doctrines are the same, including the doctrines of the Trinity, the Incarnation, and the Resurrection; so that Berdyaev, in arguing for the truths of Christianity over the truths of pure science and pure reason was arguing from many of the same premises as Western Christian intellectuals against what he perceived to be the destructive direction of the atheism of the intellectual establishment both in the Soviet Union and in the West.

I have chosen these six examples of thinkers to represent the Christian intellectuals in the 20th century—Barth, Brunner, Maritain, Marcel, Unamuno, and Berdyaev—not only because they are great thinkers and great believers, but because they perceived so acutely the epistemological weaknesses and hence the dangers of much modern thought. They all began their intellectual careers fully under the influence of the Intellectual Establishment in the 20th century, which ranges from a militant atheism in purely philosophical circles to a galloping secularism in theological circles. Ultimately they chose not to join that Establishment but to fight it, and their reasons were much the same: they recognized that the really important truths are not to be found by the unaided reason or by the unaided senses. They all perceived the crippling limitations of philosophy and science. They were convinced that man is not merely a bundle of atoms, that he does not live by bread alone, that God's word is truer than man's word, and that science and philosophy need not condemn men to a life of meaninglessness and despair when the word of God can lead them to serenity in this life and salvation in the next.

This narrow representation of Christian intellectuals cannot, of course, do justice to the strength of the influence of Christianity upon 20th-century thought, for there are dozens of other 20th-century Christian intellectuals who have compellingly stated the case for Christianity in this post-Christian age—just as there are hundreds, and more likely thousands, of other influential 20th-century intellectuals not mentioned in the previous chapter who have struck telling blows against religion and made massive contributions to the triumph of atheism.

CHAPTER IX

WHERE NOW?

Goethe was right when he observed that "the real, the deepest, the sole theme of the world and of history, that to which all others are subordinated, remains the conflict between belief and unbelief." The statement is as true now as it has been at any time in the past, despite the mounting evidence that the conflict seems to be coming to an end and that the atheistic intellectuals have won the day.

There is no denying that most intellectuals have now been pretty thoroughly de-Christianized and that they believe that religion has been effectively removed from the world of ideas. The conviction that there is no God has become in most intellectual quarters an unchallenged premise. The influence of major 20th-century defenders of Christianity, such as those discussed in the previous chapter, has not prevailed. The rationalism which began with Descartes and the scientism that began with Comte appear to have done their work. Furthermore, as we have seen, the most influential Christian intellectuals in the 20th century even up to the present time tend to spend their primary intellectual energies and talents not in challenging the Intellectual Establishment but in making concessions to it, when they are not ignoring it.

And yet the Intellectual Establishment has not won the war against Christianity because it has not yet won the epistemological battle, and what is more it may never win it. The epistemological arguments of the great 19th- and 20th-century Christian intellectuals will not go away. As we have seen, all maintained that the most important truths cannot be scientific truths because the scientific method is not capable of dealing with the truths that count most, but that religion—and specifically Christianity—can and does. Dostoevsky observed that "Reason is only reason," and he might have added, and would have been glad to add, that "Science is only science."

After two hundred years of fierce intellectual activity, especially scientific activity, de-Christianized intellectuals still cannot tell us why we were put on this earth or what we are supposed to do on it, and they never will be able to tell us. The universe and all that is in it may have been 98 percent mystery to the ancient Greeks but after the Age of Reason and the Age of Science it is still 97 percent mystery, or perhaps more nearly 99 percent mystery now.

In the face of the failure of the scientific method in solving the mysteries of existence, there is now some evidence that an era of scientific humility is beginning to set in. There is, for example, among the most thoughtful scientists a growing realization that the universe is vastly more complex than even the most imaginative scientists can suppose and that the human mind will never be able to grasp it. Every scientific discovery raises more questions than it answers.

The biologist Gunther Stent in *The Coming of the Golden Age*, for instance, is resigned to the conclusion that we will never know how the universe began or even what the most fundamental atomic particles are, that such mysteries are enclosed in a weary and ultimately endless succession of Chinese boxes. Sir Bernard Lovell, one of the world's great astronomers, has called up the famous confrontation in 1860 between Thomas Hunry Huxley and Bishop Wilberforce over the relative validity of science and religion as ultimate solutions to man's ultimate problems. Subsequent events seemed to demonstrate that Huxley was right and Wilberforce was wrong, but Lovell's conclusion suggests that the tortoise may beat out the hare after all. "We have deluded ourselves that through science we find the only answer to a true understanding about nature and the universe. The simple belief in automatic material progress by means of scientific discovery and application is a tragic myth of our age." "I cannot believe," he concludes, "that this quest for scientific understanding embraces the totality of human purpose," but rather that "the pursuit of understanding is a transcendent value in man's life and purpose." And Mr. Robert Jastrow in his recent book, *God and the Astronomers*, observes that "the scientist has scaled the mountains of ignorance; he is about to conquer the highest peak; as he pulls himself over the final rock, he is greeted by a band of theologians who have been sitting there for centuries."

Professor Everett Mendelson, a scientific historian at Harvard University, goes even further in stating flatly that "science as we know it has outlived its usefulness," and he has challenged the objectivity of the scientific method, which he concludes is not "theory-neutral," as scientists tend to insist, but indeed "theory-laden," that ultimately it is not possible to separate the scientist from the experiment. Osmond Crosby, a board member of the Institute of Noetic Sciences, also reflects the new disillusionment of scientists with science. "After being seduced for 400 years by the scientific method," he observes, "we have come to realize that science is not the only way of getting at truth and at universal solutions. There is another way. We can also look at our surroundings in ways that religion, mysticism, and philosophy have been trying to get at for a long time." And Professor Frank Rhodes, a well-known geologist, takes an even dimmer view of the claims of the scientific method. "It may be," he says, "that the qualities we measure have as little relationship to the world itself as a telephone number to its subscriber."

This increasing recognition by pure scientists of the crippling limitations of science is also being reflected in the thinking of some of the most thoughtful behavioral scientists who attempt to predict human behavior. The aims and methods of human engineering are now everywhere under scrutiny if not outright attack. The Italian psychoanalyst Robert Assagioli, for example, has concluded that "the will can be truly called the unknown and neglected factor in modern psychology, psychotherapy and education"; and the Viennese psychiatrist Viktor Frankl insists that man's will to meaning is stronger than the Freudian will to pleasure. Theodore Roszak, one of the most articulate spokesmen against the false optimism of those who place their trust in scientific rationality, has, in his book *Where the Wasteland Ends*, called for a wider recognition that spiritual knowledge and power are even more crucial to human existence than scientific knowledge and power, and that the scientific method "has succeeded not only in denaturing personal human experience but in denuding life of its mystery and sacredness."

As if in self-defense, scientists have now broadened scientific inquiry from studying matter in motion to studying the spirit in motion. Scientifically structured experiments with such phenomena as ESP and clairvoyance are becoming increasingly widespread. Biochemists and physicians are consulting faith healers in order to find out whether they know something that scientists don't. Even conservative research institutes are experimenting with the powers of the mind over the powers of matter, and federal grants in the United States now support psychic research. Parapsychology, clairvoyance, precognition, and psychokinesis appear to be achieving the dimensions of a new frontier. There is perhaps some significance too to the fact that Werner von Braun, shortly before he died, turned from rocketry to parapsychology, which he called "one of the most promising fields of modern science." Experiments which demonstrate skill in guessing correctly aginst trillion-to-one odds are enough to send any traditional scientist back to the drawing board.

These tentative scientific probings into the possibility of spiritual existence may in fact be the first steps that will lead scientists and scientific-oriented intellectuals back to religion. One might, in fact, go even further and suggest that if religion is to be restored to the intellectual community, it may be restored more effectively by scientists than by theologians; for at the very time that thoughtful scientists are coming to recognize the limitations of science and the possibility of the existence of spiritual man, theologians are now coming under the full sway of the scientific spirit. Malachi Martin captures the tenor of the writing in contemporary religious journals by pointing out that, apart from the official and professional publications of still-vibrant groups in America such as the Mormons and Jehova's Witnesses, "writing about religion itself seems now to be a matter of baboons, test tubes, cosmic flows, therapeutic suggestibility, polls and statistics, Skinnerian reinforcement, computerized data, para-psychology, social activism, and political witnessing, rather than a matter of God, salvation, the soul, sin, virtue, immortality, and spirit."

By way of contrast, scientists are now not only probing the spiritual aspects of man's nature but are even taking a serious look at the possibility of life after death as, for example, Elizabeth Kubler-Ross and Raymond Moody have been doing. Science would appear to be on the brink of investigating something of which the scientific world has for over a century denied the very existence, namely the human soul.

Thus, there is much reason to believe that the short era in which reason-and-science reigned over religion in the Western world may be coming to an end, that it was a noble experiment, but that it failed. Furthermore, man does not appear to have any merely human faculties left which could challenge his reason or his senses as a means to truth. His other noble faculties, his imagination and his memory, are powerful instruments in the search for truth, but it seems unlikely that history or literature and the arts will ever take the place of philosophy or science as the primary means to truth because they do not have the built-in authority of philosophy and science. But if pure philosophy and pure science, i.e., the reason and the senses, have also failed in man's search for the ultimate answers to the ultimate questions about life, it is almost as if there is nowhere to go except back to religion.

After all, the great question is, does God exist or does He not exist? And if He does exist has He spoken to men? Has He told them why they exist and how they ought to behave? Christianity maintains that He does exist, that He has spoken to men, that He has told them why they exist and how they ought to behave and with a degree of authority that only religion can provide.

If it is premature to say that the time is ripe for intellectuals to return to religion, it is not premature to declare the fatal limitations of scientific rationalism and hence the beginnings of the end of the Age of Science. It may be expected that more and more intellectuals will face more frankly and more realistically the basic questions of the meaning of human existence. They may begin to recognize more fully that the great truths of human existence cannot come merely from the senses or the reason but must come from sources which transcend science and philosophy and that the only source that can come close to approaching the ultimate truth is religion. They may increasingly come now to realize too that man is a spiritual creature after all, that he is not a bag of bones or atoms and that he doesn't live by bread alone. They may increasingly realize that life and the universe are mostly mystery and will always remain so, despite whatever scientific discoveries in time turn up. They may be expected to develop more intellectual humility and more spiritual humility. They may be expected, in short, to become more thoughtful thinkers.

Defenders of Christianity at the same time would do well to realize more fully that its truths have always been superior to the truths of unbelieving intellectuals and they ought to spend more of their talents and energies combating the encroachments of the scientific method upon Christianity and less on making unwarranted concessions.

At the same time it is necessary to remind ourselves that the de-Christianizing of the intellectuals has been such a long and steady process, as this study has suggested, and was built on such a broad intellectual base that it may have reached a point of no return. To take the most pessimistic view, the re-Christianizing of the intellectuals may require nothing less than the Second Coming of Christ or the First Coming of Somebody Else, and even that may not be enough.

On the other hand, it is conceivable that one of the consequences of the recognition of the limitations of science by scientists themselves is that the burden of finding the truth about the human condition may be pushed back upon the philosophers. If so, then there may come a time when the philosophers will also recognize the limitations of philosophy and human reason, and then the emphasis may shift once again back to religion. In other words, just as Comte in the 19th century saw that civilization went from Revelation to reason to science, it may be that the reverse of these steps will in time be taken. And if it is further recognized that Christianity, for all its difficulties with intellectuals and the intellectuals with it, is the best witness of the existence of God and of a personal God at that, then the re-Christianizing of the intellectuals is not an impossibility. Such a scenario is perhaps not outrageous, though it is not imminent either.

And yet belief is catching just as unbelief is catching, and if a few powerful minds perceive that the truths of God are superior to the truths of man, if they become convinced, for example, that Dostoevsky and Kierkegaard are more nearly right and that Nietzsche and Marx and Freud are more nearly wrong about religion, they may well do as much to restore religion as those great anti-religious minds have done to destroy it.

Meanwhile, until these great minds make their appearance, one can only hope that intellectuals will begin to scrutinize the doctrines and beliefs and limitations of science and reason and other purely human methods of reaching truth with at least the same degree of thoroughness as intellectuals in the past have scrutinized the doctrines and beliefs of Christianity.

INDEX

Abelard, Peter, 15, 24, 40, 41, 70
Abel, 32
Abraham, 95, 114
Adam, 32, 35
Adams, John, 128
Aeschylus, 51
Aesop, 62
Agapetus, (Pope), 21
Agricola, Rodolphus, 58
Agrippa von Nettesheim, Henricus Cornelius, 78
Aksakov, Sergei Timofeyevich, 108
Albertus Magnus, St., 25
Alberti, 57
d'Alembert, Jean le Romd, 74, 76
Alexander the Great, 16
Allen, Ethan, 126, 127, 130
Altizer, Thomas J. J., 166-69
Ambrose, St., 23
Anselm of Laon, 24, 30
Athanasius, St., 15, 20, 36
Aquinas, St. Thomas, 15, 25, 46, 47, 64, 74, 79, 150, 165, 181
Aretino, Pietro, 57
Aristophanes, 63
Aristotle, 10, 16, 26, 27, 38, 41, 50, 51, 55, 56, 70, 101, 150, 180
Arius, 35, 36
Ascham, Roger, 58, 63
Assagioli, Robert, 194
Augustine, St., 15, 20, 21, 23, 28-31, 35, 47, 54, 65, 78, 79, 181
Aurispa, Giovanni, 51
Aurelius, Marcus, 19, 70

Averroes, 26, 38, 39
Avicenna, 38, 39
Ayer, Sir Alfred, 150

Baader, Franz Xavier von, 103, 105, 187
Babbitt, Irving, 82
Bacon, Francis, 75, 84, 85, 123
Bagehot, Walter, 102
Bakunin, Mikhail, 109
Barth, Karl, 139, 163, 166, 172-79, 181, 182, 188, 189
Basil, St., 20
Bauer, Bruno, 106
Bayle, Pierre, 75
Beauchamp, Philip, 100
Bede, St., 23
Belinsky, Vissarion, 115
Bembo, Pietro, 56
ben Abraham, Rabbi Solomon, 40
Bentham, Jeremy, 15, 100, 101, 111
Berdayev, Nikolai Aleksandrovich, 186-89
Bergson, Henri, 180
Bergier, Nicholas Sylvester, 88
Berkely, Bishop George, 87, 91
Bernard, Claude, 98
Bernard of Clairvaux, St., 15, 41, 70
Bernard of Chartres, 24
Berthier, Guillaume François, 91
Biondo, Flavio, 56
Blount, Charles, 72
Bloy, Leon, 180
Boccaccio, Giovanni, 54, 55
Boerhaave, Hermann, 85

Bogdanov, Aleksandr, 186
Bolingbroke, Viscount Henry St. John, 73
Boehme, Jacob, 187
Bonald, Louis G. A., vicomte de, 96
Bonaparte, Napoleon, 16, 94
Bonaventura (St. Bonaventure), 25
Bonhoeffer, Dietrich, 158, 163, 164, 166-68, 172
Boulanger, George Ernest, 77
Bowne, Borden Parker, 126, 134
Bracciolini, Poggio, 51
Bradford, William, 122
Braun, Werner Magnus Maximilian von, 195
Brownson, Orestes, 131
Bruni, Leonardo, 55
Brunner, Emil, 172, 176-79, 182, 189
Buchanan, George, 58
Büchner, Eduard, 106, 108, 109
Budé, Guillaume, 57, 59
Buffon, Count Georges Louis Leclerc de, 85
Bultmann, Rudolf, 158-65, 168, 172
Burkhardt, Jacob, 52, 68, 105
Burke, Edmund, 82
Butler, Bishop Joseph, 87, 91
Bush, Douglas, 57

Cain, 32
Calvin, John, 14, 79, 80, 128, 131, 138, 173, 176
Camerarius, 58
Campanella, Tommaso, 56
Camus, Albert, 141-43, 146, 169, 182-84, 186
Carnap, Rudolph, 150
Casaubon, Florence Estienne Meric, 58, 59
Cassiodorus, Flavius Magnus Aurelius, 21, 23
Castiglione, Baldassare, 56
Channing, William Ellery, 126, 127, 131, 132
Charlemagne, 23, 47
Chateaubriand, Francois Renè, vicomte de, 94, 95, 110

Chernyshevsky, Nikolai, 109, 115
Christ, 28, 29, 36, 42, 54, 55, 71, 73, 80, 95, 104, 106, 117, 128, 165, 174, 175, 177, 189, 198
Chrysostom, St. John, 20, 48
Cicero, Marcus Tullius, 19, 29, 51, 54, 56, 63, 70
Clarke, James Freeman, 126, 128
Clement, St., 20
Clement of Alexandria, 33
Colet, John, 60-62
Collier, Jeremy, 81
Collins, Anthony, 72
Columbus, Christopher, 56
Comte, Auguste, 96-99, 112, 113, 191, 198
Condillac, Étienne Bonnot de, 77, 85
Condorcet, Marquis de, 77
Constantine the Great, 20, 21
Constantius, Emperor, 36
Copernicus, Nicolaus, 84
Cox, Harvey, 166
Crane, R. S. 81, 82
Creighton, James Edwin
Crosby, Osmond, 193
Cyprian, (Thascius Caecilius Cyprianus), 20

Daniel, Samuel, 64
Dante, (Alighieri), 55
Darwin, Charles Robert, 101, 102, 134-36, 154
Decius, Emperor, 33, 39
Democritus, 13
Demosthenes, 51
Descartes, René, 73-75, 102, 140, 150, 191
Dewey, John, 15, 128, 153-55, 165
Diderot, Denis, 74, 76, 77, 88, 89, 94
Dobrolyubov, Nikolai, 109
Dominic, St., 25
Donatus, (Bishop of Carthage), 35
Dostoevsky, Fyodor Mikhailovich, 108-10, 114-18, 120, 146, 156, 169, 172, 176, 184, 187, 192, 198
Duns Scotus, John, 25

Eckhart, Johannes, 25
Edwards, Jonathan, 124-27, 135
Elizabeth I, Queen, 63
Elyot, Sir Thomas, 58, 62, 63
Emerson, Ralph Waldo, 126, 127, 131-33
Engels, Friedrich, 151
Enoch, 32
Epictetus, 19, 70
Epicurus, 13
Erasmus, Desiderius, 57, 58, 60-62
Erigena, Johannes Scotus, 23
Euripides, 51
Eusebius, St., 36
Eve, 32, 35
da Feltre, Vittorino, 56, 61
Ferguson, James, Adam, 125
Feuerbach, Ludwig, 13, 106, 108, 109, 152, 157, 165
Ficino, Marsilio, 54-56
Filelfo, Franceso, 51
Fiske, John, 126, 128
Francis of Assisi, St., 25, 42, 180
Frankl, Viktor, 194
Franklin, Benjamin, 126-29
Fréron, Elie Catherine, 89, 91
Freud, Sigmund, 15, 137, 138, 148, 165, 198

Galen, 60
Galileo, 84, 85
Galvani, Luigi, 85
Gassendi, Pierre, 75
de Gerson, Jean Charlier, 30
Gibbon, Edward, 73
Gilbert, William, 84
Gladstone, William Ewart
Godwin, Charles
Goethe, Johann Wolfgang von, 103, 191
Gregory, St., (the Great), (Pope Gregory I) 23, 43
Gregory of Nyssa, St., 20
Gregory of Tours, St., 22, 23
Grimm, Friedrich Melchoir, Baron von, 77
Grocyn, William, 59, 60

Grote, George, 100
Grotius, Hugo, 58
Guarino da Verona, 56

Hamilton, William, 166, 168, 169
Harnack, Adolph von, 175, 177
Harrington, Sir John Lane, 64
Harris, William Torrey, 126, 134
Hartley, David, 125
Harvey, William, 84, 85
Hegel, Georg Wilhelm Fridrich, 13, 15, 104, 105, 107, 108, 112, 150, 153, 174, 182, 187
Heidegger, Martin, 139-41, 159
Heine, Heinrich, 103
Helvetius, Claude-Adrien, 74, 77, 88, 89
Herbert of Cherbury, Lord, 70, 71
Herodotus, 48, 51
Herschel, Sir William, 85
Hertzen, Alexander, 109
Hesiod, 63
Hilary, St., 20
Hippolytus, 20, 37
Hitler, Adolf, 16, 160, 163
Hobbes, Thomas, 75, 77, 79, 80, 102, 123, 165
Hofstadter, Richard, 124
Holbach, Paul-Henri Thiry, Baron d', 74, 77, 88, 94
Homer, 56, 63
Horace, 19
Howison, George H., 126, 132
Hume, David, 73, 83, 100, 125, 153
Husserl, Edmund, 177
Hutcheson, Francis, 125
Huxley, Sir Julian, 144-46, 148, 176
Huxley, Thomas Henry, 102, 144, 145, 154, 193

Irenaeus, St., 20, 37
Iscariot, Judas, 32
Isis, 19
Italicus, Silius, 63
Isaac, 114
Isadore, Bishop of Seville, 22
James, William, 152-54

Jaspers, Karl, 140, 141
Jastrow, Robert, 193
Jefferson, Thomas, 126-29, 132
Jenner, Edward, 85
Jerome, St., 15, 20, 23, 29, 54
John, St., 32
John, St., (of the Cross), 78, 158
John of Salisbury, 24
Johnson, Samuel, 71, 82, 87, 126, 127

Keynes, John Maynard, 14
Khomiakov, Alexei, 108, 187
Kierkegaard, Soren, 110-14, 118, 120, 139-41, 144, 146, 169, 172, 184, 185, 198
Kireyevsky, Ivan, 108
Kristeller, Paul Oscar, 57
Kubler-Ross, Elizabeth, 196

Lamarck, Chevalier de, 85, 153
Lamennais, Felicité Robert, 96
La Mettrie, Julien Offray de, 76, 77
Landriani, Gherardo, 51
Laplace, Marquis de, 85
Lavoisier, Antoine Lavrent, 85
Law, William, 87, 91
Leibnitz, Gottfried Wilhelm, 103
Lemaitre, F. E. Jules, 94
Lenin, Nikolai, 151, 152, 165
Leo X, Pope, 41, 56, 59
Linacre, Thomas, 58-60
Linnaeus, Carolus, 85
Littre, Maxmilien Paul Émile, 96-98
Livy, 19
Locke, John, 12, 71, 72, 75, 86, 103, 123, 135, 153
Lombard, Peter (Petrus Lombardus), 24
Lovell, Sir Bernard, 192
Lucan, 19, 63
Lucian, 62, 63
Lucletius (Titus Lucretius Carus), 51
Lunacharsky, Anatoli, 186
Luther, Martin, 65, 78-80, 83, 138, 165, 173, 174, 176
Lyly, William, 62

Martin, Malachi, 195
Maritain, Jacques, 139, 179-82, 188, 189
Marcion, 32, 33
Marcel, Gabriel, 139, 144, 181, 183, 184, 186, 189
Marx Karl, 12, 15, 16, 106-08, 151, 198
Mani, 43
Manetti, Gianozzo, 55
de Maistre, Joseph, 95
Maimonides, Moses, 39, 40
McCosh, James, 126, 128
Mendelson, Everett, 193
Merleau-Ponty, Maurice, 139, 143, 144
Mill, James, 101
Mill, James Stuart, 101
Milton, John, 62, 64
Mohammed, 26
Montaigne, Michel Eyguem de, 65, 72, 75
Monteney, Charles Palissot de, 89
Montanus, 34
Montesquieu, Baron de la Brede, 75
Moody, Raymond, 196
More, St. (Sir) Thomas, 46, 58-60.
Moses, 95, 104

Nebrija, Elio Antonio, 58
Nietzsche, Friedrich Wilhelm, 15, 105, 118-20, 137, 138, 140, 141, 146, 148, 150, 156, 158, 165, 169, 198
Newcomb, Simon, 126, 128
Newman, John Henry, 110, 111, 118, 120, 165, 172
Newton, Sir Isaac, 75, 84, 85, 102, 135
Niccoli, Niccolo de, 51
Nicholas, of Cusa, 58
Nicholas II, Czar, 187
Nicholas V, Pope, 56
Noah, 32
Nonnotte, Abbé, 88

de Ochis, Andreoli, 51
Origen, 20, 33
Oumansoff, Raissa, 179, 180

Ovid, 63

Paine, Thomas, 126-29
Paley, William, 99
Palmer, Elihu, 126, 127, 130
Parker, Samuel, 81
Parker, Theodore, 126, 127
Parks, Henry Bamford, 124
Parrington, Vernon L., 130
Pascal, Blaise, 74
Paul, St. 33, 176
Paissey, Father, 117
Peel, Sir Robert, 111
Peirce, Charles, Sanders, 127, 128, 152, 154
Pelagius, 35, 82
Peter, St., 95
Petronius, Gaius, 19, 51
Petrarch, Francesco, 53, 55, 78
Philo, 29
Pico Della Mirandola, 55
Pisarev, Dmitri, 109
Pius II, Pope, 56
Pius XII, Pope, 144
Plato, 16, 47, 50, 51, 54-56, 65, 70, 101, 129, 150
Plautus, Titus Maccius, 51
Plakhanov, Georgi, 186
Pliny—(the elder), 19
Pliny—(the younger), 19, 51
Plotinus, 19
Plutarch, 19, 55, 70
Polybius, 51
Popper, Sir Karl, 150
Porter, Noah, 126, 128
Priestley, Joseph, 85

Quintilian, 19

Rabelais, Francois, 65
Raleigh, Sir Walter, 65
Regensburg, Bernard von, 41
Renan, Ernest, 96, 98, 99, 157
Reuchlin, Johann, 58, 59
Rhodes, Frank, 194
Ricoeur, Paul, 141
Ritschl, Albrecht, 176, 177

Robinson, John A. T., 166-68
Roszak, Theodore, 194
Rousseau, Jean Jacques, 15, 77, 80-84, 88, 89, 130-32
Royce, Josiah, 126, 127, 134
Rozanov, Vassily, 187
146-48

St. Simon, Comte de, 13
Salutati, 51
Salvian, 48
Santayana, George, 72
Sartre, Jean Paul, 15, 139, 141-43, 146, 182-84
Satan, 33, 120
Savonarola Girolamo, 55
Scaliger, Joseph Justus, 58
Schelling, F. W. J. von, 135, 187
Schleiermacher, Friedrich D. E., 103, 105, 176, 177
Schopenhauer, Arthur, 105
Scotus, John Duns, 64
Seneca, Lucius Annaeus, 19, 70
Sewall, Samuel, 122
Shaftesbury, Third Earl of, 80, 81
Shakespeare, William, 62
Shelley, Percy Bysshe, 100
Sidney, Sir Philip, 46, 64
Sixtus IV, Pope, 56
Smith, Adam, 125
Solovyev, Sergei, 187, 188
Sophocles, 51
Spencer, Herbert, 102, 154
Spenser, Edmund, 62, 64, 136
Spinoza, Baruch, 75, 102, 103
Stalin, Joseph, 16
Stent, Gunther, 192
Stewart, Randall, 133
Strauss, David Friedrich, 106, 108, 157
Sturm, Johannes, 61
Sylvester, Bernard, 24

Tacitus, Publius, Cornelius, 19, 51
Taine, Adolf, Hyppolyte, 96, 98
Tertullian, 20, 28, 34, 48, 78, 79
Thomasius, Christian, 103, 105
Thoreau, Henry David, 126, 127

Thucydides, 48, 51
Tillich, Paul Johannes, 10, 158, 160-63, 165, 167, 172
Tillotson, John, 72, 81
Tindal, Matthew, 72, 73, 87
Toland, John, 72
Tolstoy, Leo, 108, 109, 121, 162, 187
Traversari, Ambrogio, 55

Unamuno, Miquel de, 183-86, 189

Vahanian, Gabriel, 166
Valdés, Juan de, 58, 59
Valla, Lorenzo, 57
Van Buren, Paul M., 166
Vincent of Beauvais, 24
Virgil, 19, 56, 63
Vitruvius Pollio, Marcus, 51
Vives, Juan Luis, 58
Vogt, Karl Christopher, 106, 108, 109

Volta Count Alessandro, 85
Voltaire, 12-15, 73-75, 88, 89

Waldo, Peter, 42
Warburton, Bishop, William, 87
Wesley, John, 87
Whichcote, Benjamin, 81
Whitefield, George, 124
Whitehead, Alfred North, 144, 146
Whitman, Walt, 126, 127, 133
Wilberforce, Bishop William, 145, 193
William of Ockham, 25
Witherspoon, John, 126, 127
Wittgenstein, Ludwig, 148, 166
Wollaston, William Hyde, 73
Woodbridge, Fredrick J. E.
Woolman, John, 126, 127

Zwingli, Ulrich, 14

From the same publisher:

Dynamics of World History by Christopher Dawson. 509 pages. Paper. $7.95.
Christianity in East and West by Christopher Dawson. Paper: $4.95.
Escape from Scepticism: Liberal Education as if Truth Mattered by Christopher Derrick. Paper: $2.95.
Joy Without a Cause: Selected Essays of Christopher Derrick. Paper: $4.95.
Beyond Détente: Toward an American Foreign Policy by Paul Eidelberg. Cloth: $12.95.
A Better Guide Than Reason: Studies in the American Revolution by M. E. Bradford. Cloth: $12.95; paper: $4.95.
Citizen of Rome: Reflections from the Life of a Roman Catholic by Frederick D. Wilhelmsen. 345 pages. Paper: $5.95.
The Prophetic Poet and the Spirit of the Age: Volume I: *Why Flannery O'Connor Stayed Home* by Marion Montgomery. 488 pages. Cloth: $19.95. Volume II: *Why Poe Drank Liquor.* Cloth: $19.95. Volume III: *Why Hawthorne Was Melancholy.* Cloth: $19.95.
The Impatience of Job by George W. Rutler. Paper: $3.95.
Generations of the Faithful Heart: On the Literature of the South. By M. E. Bradford. 216 pages. Paper: $5.95.
Christianity and the Intellectuals. By Arther Trace. 206 pages. Paper: $4.95.
Angels, Apes, and Men. By Stanley L. Jaki. Paper: $4.50.
Classic European Short Stories. Robert Beum (ed.) 278 pages. Paper: $5.95.
Enemies of the Permanent Things: Observations of Enormity in Politics and Literature. By Russell Kirk. 309 pages. Paper: $7.95.
Eliot and His Age: T. S. Eliot's Moral Imagination in the Twentieth Century. By Russell Kirk. 476 pages. Paper: $9.95.

(All prices include postage & handling.)